WOMEN'S VOICES

Global Perspectives on the Right to Vote

Linda Strite Murnane, Renee Dopplick, and Caryl Ben Basat
EDITORS

AMERICAN BAR ASSOCIATION
International Law Section

Cover design by Monica Alejo/ABA Design

Printed in the United States of America.

26 25 24 23 22   5 4 3 2 1

A catalog record for this book is available from the Library of Congress.

Discounts are available for books ordered in bulk. Special consideration is given to state bars, CLE programs, and other bar-related organizations. Inquire at Book Publishing, ABA Publishing, American Bar Association, 321 N. Clark Street, Chicago, Illinois 60654-7598.

www.shopABA.org

Contents

Foreword

U.S. Ambassador Prudence Bushnell (retired)

Fifteen authors from ten countries describe efforts to secure women's right to vote and the related effects over the past century. Contributing authors brilliantly outline what has been accomplished and what tasks remain to close political gender gaps. They underscore the transformational leadership role women have played to achieve gains that all of us, women and men, enjoy today.

I am seized by these narratives and their recommendations. None of the countries or nations mentioned, with the exception of the Iroquois Confederacy tribal nation, empowered women to participate politically at the beginning of the 20th century. It took women's leadership, strategies, and perseverance over decades to secure the electoral rights we have today. The legal right to vote, however, has not guaranteed women's meaningful inclusion in political parties, elected positions, and leadership positions. Challenges remain. Women are still underrepresented in political positions and within decision-making processes at all levels of governance. Further, women have yet to become equal partners in the public and private sectors, much less equally paid partners.

Although the writers seldom use the word "leadership," it resonates as the source of the change and persistence. If one considers every problem or barrier to be a leadership opportunity, prospects abound. Momentum for positive change is underway. The "Me Too" and Black Lives Matter movements are global. The COVID-19 pandemic clearly exposed structural gender inequities, particularly in women's roles on the frontlines of the pandemic response as essential health care and education workers and at home as the primary caregivers of children and families. These profound societal disruptions create an extraordinary opportunity to innovate responses and to put gender equality and empowerment of women at the core of our future.

Within this book, the authors draw upon history and their own experiences to highlight actions we can use to accomplish positive change. Women leaders at international, national, and local levels are showing what effectiveness looks like in the face of overwhelming challenges. The increased media attention on women leaders and their accomplishments is in and of itself a positive change in our world because it recognizes women's influence and other aspects of leadership.

My experience as a diplomat and ambassador required transformational leadership in action. I have promoted leadership, among women especially, ever since I realized that it is neither a genetically endowed male characteristic nor a process limited to those in power. My style of leadership focuses on shared values and group efforts to create a better future. I introduced leadership training to the State Department in the 1980s and put leadership into practice as Deputy Assistant Secretary in the Bureau of African Affairs, Ambassador to the Republic of Kenya and to the Republic of Guatemala in the 1990s, and dean of the Leadership and Management School of the Foreign Service Institute in the 2000s. When al Qaida blew up the U.S. embassy in Nairobi during my term as U.S. Ambassador to Kenya, the transformational leadership demonstrated at every level by Americans and Kenyans to unite and rebuild further convinced me that a focus on people and their empowerment is essential to peaceful and inclusive development and long-term prosperity.

Building on these experiences, almost ten years ago, I founded a leadership institute at a liberal arts college on the notion that inclusive political and societal leadership will not occur by accident. Rather, critical leadership skills can empower and inspire excellence, diversity, inclusion, and ethical leadership in public service.

Courage is gender neutral. We are at a historical turning point to transform the pandemic's recovery into meaningful opportunities to end violence against women, effectively address and overcome persistent barriers to equality, and value women in decision-making at all levels so that they have input on issues that affect their lives, families, communities, and the world we share. Nothing just happens. Now is an important time for courage, cooperation, and transformative leadership. Our generation and future generations of women and girls are depending on us.

As these chapters illustrate, we need action to advance gender equality and to strengthen women's legal rights and their empowerment to engage in economic, social, and political life. We need to eliminate a variety of discriminatory barriers, particularly for women of color and Native and Indigenous women, and significantly increase the representation of women in political power, institutions of governance, and decision-making in public life.

All of us play a role in making it happen. Occupying a formal political or policy position as a "leader" is not a prerequisite to influencing others to achieve common goals. Most of the women and men who courageously and successfully struggled for women's right to vote and women's rights generally over generations never held high office. They leave us permission to build on their successes from where we find ourselves today, never mind age, race, economic status, citizenship, or gender. They leave us challenges to be remembered when authors 100 years from now review our contributions. Most importantly, they serve as role models. They thought strategically, acted intentionally, and demonstrated courage. So can we.

Prudence Bushnell
United States Ambassador (retired)
Recipient of the Francis Shattuck Security and Peace Award 2019–2020
from the American Bar Association International Law Section

Preface

Colonel Linda Strite Murnane

Women's right to vote has been global. This book celebrates a century of progress for women's voting rights and offers thought-leadership on challenges and opportunities for fully realizing gender equality and women's empowerment, particularly their full and meaningful inclusion in political life and leadership.

This book arose from the 100th anniversary of women's right to vote in the United States, as enacted by the 19th Amendment to the U.S. Constitution on August 26, 1920. As part of the centennial celebrations, I offered to coordinate a special global collection of essays for publication by the ABA International Law Section as a companion to personal stories about the importance of the right to vote by women in several countries captured on video and produced with the assistance of LexisNexis and the International Foundation for Electoral Systems (IFES).

These essays will be of particular interest for advocates of women's voting rights and political inclusion. They provide insightful and pragmatic best practices and suggested actions for women's rights advocates, policy leaders, legislators, political party leaders, and lawyers to remove bias, prejudice, and discriminatory practices in political parties, elections, and public life.

The editorial board of this book felt it was important to include in this work those stories that remind us of the importance of protecting, promoting, and upholding the right to vote as a fundamental right and how that right is closely tied with gender equality and women's empowerment to engage in public and political life.

The authors illustrate how the right to vote is a crucial step but not the only step for achieving women's full participation at the polls, in political parties, and as candidates in countries around the world. Historical legal and local restrictions to the right to vote in some countries, including the United States, impeded political equality by marginalizing categories of voters for decades based on education levels; marital status; and Native, Indigenous, racial, and ethnic identity. The right to vote also does not denote full political inclusion. Even now, women remain underrepresented in legislatures worldwide, with a global average of 26.1 percent of national parliament seats held by women in 2021, according to the Inter-Parliamentary Union.

We are now once again in a historic period for women's rights and equality, marked by milestone celebrations of suffrage in several countries and the extraordinary challenge of a pandemic in a globalized world.

The global success of women depended 100 years ago, as it does now, on women organizing, networking, mobilizing, and supporting each other's efforts across borders. Reflecting on the century of women's long road to political participation and leadership, the authors explore the themes of progress thus far in legal and constitutional protections, barriers to women's inclusion in political parties, dynamics impeding women's involvement as candidates for public office, and ways to close persistent political gender gaps.

The authors of these essays represent voices from every continent, except Antarctica. The authors were chosen for their diverse perspectives and for a comparison of experiences within varied legal traditions and systems, including common law, civil law, Islamic law, and customary law. These trailblazing women agreed to share stories of triumph and challenge, whether of their own experiences or those of their mothers and grandmothers, and their thoughts on the way forward. As a reflection of their voices, the essays retain each author's use of the terms "female" and "women."

The authors wrote these essays as the world entered into a pandemic. The pandemic's disproportionate impacts on women now threaten to reverse decades, if not a century, of gains for women's legal rights and for their social, economic, and political inclusion. These impacts are worsening the unique challenges faced by women of color and Native and Indigenous women. We cannot risk reversals of important and hard-fought gains for women's rights and inclusion, not just for women as half the world's population but also for the advancement of all societies.

The essays show a global legacy of courageous efforts by women and men who advocated for women's rights and shattered barriers impeding women's ability to vote, run for elected office, and serve in political leadership. Yet, as the essays illustrate, we need further progress to strengthen women's rights, ensure gender equality, end violence against women, and achieve women's full inclusion in all aspects of life.

With the pandemic, a common phrase is that we need to "build back better." Fundamental to those efforts is the importance of ensuring that women and men enjoy the equal benefits of legal rights, participation in institutions of governance, protections from discrimination and abuses, and opportunities to thrive in their livelihoods and well-being.

We must ensure that our societies are inclusive of all persons. We must work to end bias, prejudice, and discrimination based on gender, race, ethnicity, gender and sexual orientation, religion, and other identity status that drives social and political exclusion.

I hope you enjoy reading these perspectives and feel motivated to take action to increase women's political participation and full inclusion in society as an integral part of building sustainable, responsive, and resilient prosperity. People around the world and future generations are depending on us to ensure democratic rights and freedoms, equality, and good governance through the rule of law. Now is the time to make our legacy.

Acknowledgments

Colonel Linda Strite Murnane

I am grateful to many people who made this milestone book on women's voting rights around the world possible. This book was the result of the work of a team of dedicated friends and colleagues whose vision of capturing these essays on the importance of the struggle for women's rights never strayed. Despite a global pandemic and the extraordinary challenges it imposed on each of these individuals, together we captured history, placed that history in the context of a world in transition, and illuminated paths forward for the current women's rights movement.

Within these essays, the authors have shared not just the constitutional and legal frameworks for women's voting rights and political participation within their own societies but also numerous personal perspectives from their lives and the journeys of their mothers and grandmothers. These treasured insights provide context for how the legal and political status of women have affected them, their families, and their societies, reminding us how a woman's right to vote is not to be taken for granted. I deeply thank each of the authors for her willingness to share these personal stories and insights, in her own voice.

Producing this book spanned three years under the leadership of ABA International Law Section Chairs Lisa Ryan (2019–2020), Joseph L. Raia (2020–2021), and Nancy Kaymar Stafford (2021–2022), and ABA Presidents Judy Perry Martinez (2019–2020), Patricia Lee Refo (2020–2021), and Reginald Turner (2021–2022), whose thematic public outreach topics included, in part, voting rights, the centennial anniversary in 2020 of women's voting rights granted by the 19th Amendment to the U.S. Constitution, and the role we all play in creating more just, fair, inclusive, and equitable societies grounded in the rule of law.

As part of the centennial anniversary of women's suffrage in the United States, special thanks to ABA International Law Section Chair Lisa Ryan and former Chair Gabrielle Buckley (2013–2014), whose thoughtful vision and leadership drove a year-long series of programs and activities exploring women's suffrage around the world. As part of that commemoration, the ABA International Law Section produced a collection of videos from women worldwide speaking about what it has meant to them to be free to exercise the right to cast a vote, be politically active, and serve as elected officials. The video project would not have been possible without the aid of our extraordinary partners at LexisNexis, led by Afsoon McClellan, and the International Foundation for Electoral Systems (IFES), led by Chad Vickery.

I am grateful to Renee Dopplick, whose knowledgeable support, multilingual legal research, and substantive review strengthened the book.

As ABA International Law Section Publications Officer, Caryl Ben Basat (2020–2022) effectively guided and supported this collaborative project from scoping to publication, and Clifford Sosnow (2018–2020) guided its inception. Throughout the process, sound advice and ongoing support came from staff members of the ABA International Law Section and ABA Publishing.

Thank you to the ABA Commission on Women in the Profession, led by Chair Stephanie Scharf (2019–2020) and Maureen Mulligan (2020–2021), and to the ABA International Law Section's Women's Interest Network Committee, led by Co-Chairs Judge Delissa Ridgway and Salli Swartz (2019–2020) and Gabrielle Buckley and Dana Katz (2020–2021), for their activities in support of the centennial anniversary of the 19th Amendment, as well as their ongoing activities to advance gender equality, women's legal rights, and women's inclusion in the legal and justice sectors.

I am also grateful to the women and men in countries where I had the honor to work whose courage in exercising the right to vote should inspire all of us.

To my family, thank you for encouraging and inspiring me. I am forever thankful for the trip our family made when I was in eighth grade to tour the United Nations headquarters in New York City. That experience infused me with enthusiasm for multiculturalism and for wanting to take an active role in global affairs, peace, justice, and human rights. My husband Kevin, I am deeply thankful for our marvelous adventures and the unique and loving journey we have traveled together as equals. To my daughters, Christina and Rachel, and my three grandchildren, I could not be prouder. You remind me daily of courage, determination, compassion, and capacity to inspire others.

About the Editors

Colonel Linda Strite Murnane (retired) served for nearly 30 years on active duty with the U.S. Air Force. In her Air Force career, Colonel Murnane served in a variety of positions, including ten years as a chief circuit military judge, or military judge. She presided at the first criminal trials for the U.S. Air Force during Operations Iraqi and Enduring Freedom in the war zone. Her military decorations include the Legion of Merit and the Meritorious Service Medal with bronze and silver oak leaf cluster.

She served as Chief, Court Management Services Section, at the Special Tribunal for Lebanon in the Netherlands from 2014 until her retirement in May 2017. She served as the Senior Legal Officer for Trial Chamber III, the Chief Court Management Services Section, and as Acting Head of Chambers and Acting Deputy Registrar at the International Criminal Tribunal for the former Yugoslavia (2006–2008, 2009–2012).

Colonel Murnane serves on the ABA House of Delegates as a Representative for the National Conference of Specialized Jurisdiction Court Judges and on the International Law Section Council. She is a past chair of the ABA Judicial Division.

She received the ABA Margaret Brent Women Lawyers of Achievement Award in 2008 in recognition for achieving professional excellence in the legal field and for her significant contributions for advancing women in the law. Margaret Brent was the first woman lawyer in the United States.

She received the Ohio State Bar Association Nettie Cronise Lutes Award in 2003 for opening doors for women and girls in the field of law.

Renee Dopplick is an attorney and an experienced senior executive with a background in global nonprofits and the corporate sector, working in the areas of policy, technology, and the law. Renee began her career working with Fortune 500 companies in the technology and financial sectors. Her legal practice expanded into digital tech law, including artificial intelligence and cybersecurity. She has worked in Africa, Asia/Pacific, Europe, and North America. Renee is the ABA Representative to the United Nations Economic and Social Council, the Rule of Law Officer for the

ABA International Law Section, a fellow of the American Bar Foundation, and previous Editor in Chief of *International Law News*, published by the ABA International Law Section. She has published and been a frequent speaker on tech law-related topics to a variety of domestic and international audiences. Among her publications, Renee was co-author of the chapter on AI and Legal Practice Management in the DRI AI Working Group report. Renee earned her JD degree with honors and an award from Georgetown University Law Center, an MS degree from Michigan State University, and a BS degree from the University of California, Los Angeles. She is licensed to practice law before the U.S. Supreme Court and in the courts of Washington, D.C., and Maryland.

Caryl Ben Basat is a corporate lawyer with more than 25 years of experience in mergers and acquisitions and complex cross-border equipment finance transactions worth billions of dollars. Before establishing her own firm, she spent many years practicing in large top-tier international law firms and in-house with two European aircraft leasing companies. Caryl earned her JD degree cum laude from Pace University School of Law where she served as Editor in Chief of the *Pace International Law Review* and where she also earned certificates in international law and international trade law. She earned her BA degree in English magna cum laude from San Francisco State University.

Caryl currently serves as the ABA International Law Section's Publications Officer, with responsibility for overseeing the publication and promotion of books, *International Law News*, and two law reviews published by the International Law Section in cooperation with SMU Dedman School of Law, *The International Lawyer* and *The Year in Review*.

Caryl is committed to using her skills and expertise to assist in the transition from fossil fuels to renewable energy sources. She is also passionate about promoting diversity, equity, and inclusion generally and about expanding the role of women in leadership in both the public and private sectors.

About the Contributors

Lisa L. Atkinson (Northern Cherokee/Osage) is a proud graduate of Oregon State University (BA cum laude, political science (Spanish Minor); BA cum laude, international studies (French studies emphasis)), and of the University of Washington School of Law (environmental concentration). Judge Atkinson maintains a private law practice while also serving and having served at every level (administrative, trial, and appellate) in more than 40 tribal courts throughout the United States over the past 20+ years.

Judge Atkinson has served in several leadership roles for the ABA's Tribal Courts Council, National Conference of Specialized Court Judges, GP Solo's Diversity Board, Legal Opportunities Scholarship Committee, and other important ABA committees.

Judge Atkinson has spoken at more than 20 state/national/international events on Indian law subjects, including issues of training and practice in tribal courts, domestic violence, the Indian Child Welfare Act, diversity in the legal profession, tribal Violence Against Women Act provisions, human trafficking in the casino industry, and voter disenfranchisement. Judge Atkinson has also published multiple articles on Indian law topics.

Judge Atkinson was born and raised in Oregon as the proud daughter of two retired educators, who continue to inspire her in her more than 14-year teaching career at community college and undergraduate levels.

The Honorable Margaret Beazley, AC, KC, is the 39th governor of New South Wales, commencing her five-year tenure on May 2, 2019. Prior to her appointment as governor, she enjoyed a long and distinguished law career spanning 43 years, during which time she served as a role model for women in the law at both the state and national levels. Appointed Queen's Counsel in 1989, in 1993, she was made a judge of the Federal Court of Australia, the first woman to sit exclusively in that court. In 1996, she achieved the distinction of being the first woman appointed to the New South Wales Court of Appeal and, subsequently, as the first woman to be appointed as its president. She served, on a number of occasions, as administrator of the government of the state of New South Wales. She was made a Companion of the Order of Australia in the Australia Day Honours List on January 26, 2020, for "eminent service to the people of New South Wales, particularly through leadership roles in the judiciary, and as a mentor of young women lawyers." The governor regularly publishes papers and book chapters and gives speeches on a wide range of legal topics.

Christina Blacklaws is a former president of the Law Society of England and Wales. She is an innovator in the legal field, having developed and managed one of the first "virtual" law firms and set up the UK's very first Alternative Business Structure with the Cooperative Group. She was also one of the first Directors of Innovation at a top UK firm.

She now runs her own consultancy business, providing strategic advice, particularly in the areas of transformational change, technological developments, and diversity and inclusion and holds three nonexecutive directorships in the legal field. Christina also chairs two UK government bodies in lawtech.

Christina is on the editorial board of *Legal Women*, previously represented the Women Lawyers Division on the Law Society Council, and campaigns for gender equity in the legal profession. She is the UK representative on the International Bar Association Council and a board member of the World Law Foundation and chair of the English Chapter of the World Jurist Association. Christina is a member of the Queen's Counsel Selection Panel. She is an authoritative speaker, writer, and influencer on many legal issues.

Paulette Brown is the first woman of color to lead the American Bar Association (ABA), as its president, in its history. Her presidential initiatives, through her Diversity & Inclusion 360 Commission, resulted in seven major policies developed and approved by the ABA, having a long-lasting impact on diversity and inclusion in the legal profession and the justice system. Brown simultaneously served as the first person of color to chair the Labor and Employment Section of the New Jersey State Bar Association.

Brown is also a past president of the National Bar Association (NBA). Brown is founder and principal of MindSetPower, LLC, and a former partner and Chief Diversity and Inclusion Officer of an Am Law 100 firm. She is nationally recognized for her dedication and efforts relating to diversity, equity, and inclusion, including the impact of implicit bias, and is a frequent speaker and educator on both. Brown is the co-author of two ground-breaking reports, "Visible Invisibility: Women of Color in Law Firms" and "Left Out and Left Behind: The Hurdles, Hassles and Heartaches of Achieving Long-Term Legal Careers for Women of Color."

Brown is a graduate of Howard University and Seton Hall University School of Law and has won numerous awards and honors, including the American Bar Association Margaret Brent Women Lawyers of Achievement Award and the C. Francis Stratford Award, the highest award conferred by the NBA.

U.S. Ambassador Prudence Bushnell, retired, served as Deputy Assistant Secretary of State for African Affairs (1993–1996), ambassador to the Republics of Kenya (1996–1999) and Guatemala (1999–2002), and dean of the Leadership and Management School at the Foreign Service Institute (2002–2005). Her 24-year diplomatic career informs her work as consultant, public speaker, and visiting professor on international and leadership issues. Ambassador Bushnell's achievements have been recognized through numerous U.S. Department of State awards, the U.S. Department of Commerce Peace through Commerce Award, the ABA International Law Section's Francis Shattuck Security and Peace Award, the International Women's Associates of Chicago's Rising Voice of Women Award, and three honorary doctoral degrees. Her leadership efforts to bring attention to the 1994 genocide in Rwanda were featured in the 2005 film, *Sometimes in April*. Her book *Terrorism, Betrayal, and Resilience: My Story of the 1998 U.S. Embassy Bombings* is part of the ADST-DACOR Diplomats and Diplomacy book series to increase awareness of extraordinary diplomats of the U.S. Foreign Service and their involvement in world history. She was educated in Germany, France, Pakistan, and Iran. She and her husband, Richard Buckley, an author and playwright, live in the Washington, D.C., area.

Elizabeth Chapman is a graduate lawyer and research assistant to the Honorable Margaret Beazley, AC, KC, governor of New South Wales. She has a Bachelor of Art Theory/Arts (Hon.) and JD from UNSW.

Hayashi Yoko is a legal practitioner in Tokyo, Japan. She has served as a legal counsel to women's rights organizations including the Tokyo Rape Crisis Center. As a women's human rights expert, she has established important case law on gender equality in the domestic courts in Japan.

Hayashi was a visiting professor of Waseda Law School in Tokyo (2004–2009) where she was responsible for a legal clinic on gender and law. She was an alternate member of the UN Sub-Commission on the Promotion and Protection of Human Rights (2004–2006) and a member of the Committee on the Elimination of Discrimination Against Women (CEDAW, 2008–2018), and served as its chairperson (2015–2017). Her main publication is *Implementation of the Convention on the Elimination of Discrimination Against Women in Japan* (Vol. 6, No. 2, *Journal of East Asia and International Law*, 2013).

Rachel Irura holds an LLM degree in human rights and democratization in Africa from the Centre for Human Rights, University of Pretoria, South Africa. She is the head of the Witness Support and Protection Unit (WISP) of the United Nations International Residual Mechanism for Criminal Tribunals (Mechanism). In her most recent prior position, Rachel worked as a Legal Officer (Courtroom Coordinator) for the Special Tribunal for Lebanon (STL) in the Court Management Services Section (CMSS) of the Registry in The Hague, the Netherlands. Prior to this position, she was the only Court Officer for the Special Court for Sierra Leone (SCSL), The Hague Sub-Office, the Netherlands, in the trial of the former president of Liberia Charles Taylor. Rachel has field experience as a human rights officer for the United Nations Mission in Liberia (UNMIL). Rachel has participated as a judge at various International Moot Court Competitions organized by the International Criminal Court (ICC) and the International Committee of the Red Cross (ICRC). Rachel spoke on the intersection of women's rights, health, education, and violence at recent conferences of the ABA International Law Section and the Federal Bar Association and as part of the Day at the United Nations with the National Association of Women Judges.

Carla Amaral de Andrade Junqueira is the founder and managing partner of Carla Junqueira & Associadas—CJA Trade Law. She has PhDs in economic law from Faculdade de Direito da Universidade de São Paulo (USP) and the University of Paris I: Panthéon-Sorbonne, and a master of economic law from the University of Paris I: Panthéon-Sorbonne. She specializes in economic law and assists clients in trade remedy proceedings, WTO law, customs procedures, regulatory cases, and government relations. She is an experienced lawyer with more than 20 years of experience assisting clients in more than 40 antidumping investigations in Brazil and Argentina. She is listed in the Brazilian list of the WTO Dispute Settlements panelists, and she is ranked as a leading lawyer in the legal directories of Chambers & Partners, Latin Lawyer, Legal 500, Who's Who Legal, Best Lawyers, and Practical Law Guide.

María Isabel Luján Zilbermann is a founding partner of the law firm ALTA QIL+4 Abogados in Guatemala. Her practice areas include international business transactions, mergers and acquisitions, strategic alliances, corporate restructuring involving different jurisdictions, and shareholders' agreements of local and international investors. María Isabel has also served for more than a decade as a board of directors' member and advisor in several corporations. Additionally, she provides pro bono legal assistance to institutions that promote the development of Guatemala and the enhancement of its justice system. She is the founder and current president of the Fundación Pro Bono Guatemala, a member of the Board of Trustees of La Fundación para el Desarrollo de Guatemala–FUNDESA, a member of the Aspen Global Leadership Initiative (AGLN) of the Aspen Institute, a member of the Board of Directors and former president of Fundación Vital Voices (Guatemala Chapter), and cofounder and member of the Board of Directors of Fundación Proyecto de Vida. She earned an LLM from Vrije Universiteit Brussel (VUB), Brussels, Belgium, in 1997; an LLM from New York University (NYU) School of Law as a Fulbright Scholar in 1995; and her law degree from Francisco Marroquín University Law School in Guatemala in 1993.

Fernanda Monzón Arroyo is an associate at ALTA QIL+4 Abogados. As a law student at the Universidad Francisco Marroquín (UFM) in Guatemala, Fernanda participated actively in the promotion and study of private international law as a member of UFM's winning team of the International Investment Arbitration Moot Court (*Competencia de Arbitraje Internacional de Inversión*) of American University's Washington College of Law in Washington, D.C., and a cofounder of the International Law Students Association chapter in Guatemala. Since joining ALTA QIL+4 Abogados, she has focused her practice on local and cross border transactions in business structuring, the service industry, and real estate businesses.

Alejandra Mora Mora is the Executive Secretary of the Inter-American Commission of Women (CIM) of the Organization of American States (OAS).

A Costa Rican jurist, feminist, researcher, academic, and politician, Alejandra is highly recognized in the international community for her activism for the human rights of women and girls. Prior to assuming her current position at the OAS on August 16, 2019, she served as Minister for the Status of Women and President of the National Institute of Women (INAMU) of Costa Rica, from 2014 to 2018, and Director of the Office for Women of the Office of the Ombudsperson of Costa Rica until August 2019.

She has a law degree from the University of Costa Rica (1989) and completed specialization courses at the University of Lund and Raul

Wallenberg in Sweden in 1997. She obtained her master's degree in constitutional law from the State Open University of Costa Rica in 2004 and a postgraduate degree in human rights from the University of Chile in 2007. She is the author of a book and multiple articles on different aspects of women's human rights.

Shima Rostami is a human rights and social justice activist who received her doctorate in educational leadership. Her doctoral study focused on "Developing Moral Education to Combat Human Trafficking." Currently, she serves as Executive Director of Gateway Human Trafficking (GHT), a nonprofit committed to educating communities and inspiring positive systemic change to end human trafficking. Additionally, she is an adjunct faculty member at the University of Missouri in St. Louis (UMSL) in the Department of Sociology. Besides her academic background, she has experience working with several agencies affiliated with the humanities and humanitarian efforts, including the American Red Cross of the Greater St. Louis Area where they received the International Services Award for their outstanding International Humanitarian Law (IHL) project known as Raid Cross. She has also served as a cabinet, board, and general member of numerous organizations. She is also a member of the U.S. Attorney's Human Trafficking and Hate Crime Task Forces of the Eastern District of Missouri.

Lisa Ryan is a partner at Fragomen, where she manages worldwide immigration programs for companies at every stage of growth, from startups to the Fortune 100. She is a former chair of the ABA International Law Section (2019–2020). During her tenure with the law firm, Lisa has managed the firm's U.S.-based global operations, as well as all aspects of U.S. business immigration, including nonimmigrant visas; permanent residence; citizenship; I-9 compliance; and immigration support for corporate restructuring, downsizings, and mergers and acquisitions. Lisa has represented multinational corporate clients in a variety of industries such as information technology and telecommunications, financial services, insurance/reinsurance, human resources and management consulting, manufacturing, media, commercial aviation, oil and gas, accounting, marketing/advertising, beverages, and pharmaceuticals. She has also represented numerous small to mid-sized companies, startups, and high-net-worth individuals. Lisa is a frequent speaker on business immigration topics. She also makes numerous presentations to corporate clients on immigration compliance, training, and program development. She writes and speaks on a range of issues affecting women lawyers and women in business. As chair of the International Law Section, she spearheaded the Section's centennial commemoration of the 19th Amendment and the vision for this book. Lisa speaks English and Italian. She was the founder of the *Tulane Journal of International and Comparative Law.*

Gail Heriot Silverman is a retired attorney living in Charleston, South Carolina. She earned her BA degree from Clemson University. After teaching elementary special education for two years, she began law school at the University of the Pacific, McGeorge School of Law in Sacramento, California. Following her admission to the practice of law, she worked for the California Attorney General until she was commissioned in the U.S. Air Force as a member of the Judge Advocate General's Department. Her active-duty service ended in 1982, and she continued her service as a member of the U.S. Air Force Reserve, retiring in 2004 in the grade of colonel.

Ms. Silverman practiced family law in North Carolina before returning to government service as a civilian, first as an attorney-advisor at Charleston AFB and later with the Navy Office of General Counsel. Her duties included the supervision of a government legal office practicing primarily in the areas of federal contracts and personnel law. She continued her professional activities, becoming a certified mediator. She served in the Navy's Alternative Dispute Resolution Program, and as a mentor-mediator.

In 2011, Ms. Silverman retired from federal service, but continued her engagement in the legal community through mediation and teaching. She has taught many law-related courses at both the undergraduate and graduate levels.

Priti Suri, founder and managing partner at PSA (Priti Suri & Associates), a full service law firm in India, is a seasoned lawyer with more than 35 years of experience on three continents. She developed the firm and represents its international and domestic clients, both public and privately held organizations, on a wide range of transactional matters, including a full range of cross-border M&A, strategic investments, corporate, commercial, and competition law. An active member of the international bar, Priti is currently on the Board of the International Technology Law Association. She chaired the India Committee of the ABA International Law Section for two years. In addition, she is an officer of the Inter-Pacific Bar Association and current Chair of its Publications Committee. She also led its Women Business Lawyers' Committee for four years. Priti has been consecutively rated as one of India's top 100 lawyers by *India Business Law Journal* since 2016 and was also honored with the Mayre

Rasmussen Award for the Advancement of Women in International Law by the ABA International Law Section in April 2017. Priti remains deeply engaged to ensure that young women who want to practice international law have a platform to do so and, to that end, has been instrumental in advancing gender sensitization and equality while promoting the sustainability of women in the law.

Arya Tripathy is a partner at PSA and specializes in general corporate, M&A, employment, and data protection laws. She has worked closely with various domestic and international clients on diverse aspects of business law and aims to aid in the establishment of good governance structures. She is qualified as a Certified International Privacy Professional/ Asia. Arya volunteers as the co-chair of the Delhi KnowledgeNet Chapter of the International Association of Privacy Professionals, and the vice chair of the IWIN Committee of the International Technology Law Association. She leads the firm's pro bono practice and works closely with social impact organizations aiming toward poverty alleviation, gender equality, education, health care, and sustainable development. Arya frequently writes on technology and privacy law topics, speaks at national and international events, and works with tech think tanks on evolving technology laws and policies.

Introduction

Lisa Ryan

For centuries, women around the world have been searching for their voices and equality in terms of being heard and valued. This series of essays from women around the world provides us with insights into the history of and legislation surrounding women's right to vote in their respective jurisdictions. They share their views on the continued challenges to achieving gender equality in political participation, inspirational stories of the incredible efforts being made by many to give every woman a voice in her future, and ideas for us to consider to bring society closer to true equality.

This book's unique collection of women's voices was inspired by the centennial anniversary of women's suffrage in the United States in 2020 and the 40th anniversary of the entry into force of a leading international treaty for women's rights, the Convention on the Elimination of All Forms of Discrimination Against Women (CEDAW), in 2021. These essays were written during a global pandemic and during a historic wave of transnational social activism to address gender, racial, social, and economic inequalities.

The ratification of the 19th Amendment to the U.S. Constitution in 1920, granting women the right to vote, represents one of the most significant milestones in women's journey in the United States. "This anniversary reminds us that the struggle to ensure voting rights for all Americans continues and that our voting rights should never be taken for granted," said then-**ABA President Patricia Lee Refo** on the centennial in 2020.[1]

This journey, while imperfect, has embodied the perseverance and dedication of so many to provide a breakthrough for women's voices to be recognized and counted, and for women to take an active part in shaping our country and a government that represents us, our needs, our values, and our priorities. As retired **Colonel Gail Heriot Silverman** reminds

1. Statement of ABA President Patricia Lee Refo Re: 100th Anniversary of the 19th Amendment (Aug. 18, 2020), https://www.americanbar.org/news/abanews/aba-news-archives/2020/08/statement-of-aba-president-patricia-lee-refo-re--100th-anniversa/.

us in her essay, however, this desire for full gender equality and inclusion did not begin with the 19th Amendment; rather, it started during the country's founding and remains unfulfilled.

Major strides have been made since the 19th Amendment's passage to bring greater equality in voting rights and political participation, but, even now—more than 100 years later—significant barriers to enabling every woman who wishes to have a say in her representation remain.

As with many historic events, there are vastly different views on whether the passage of the 19th Amendment is something to be truly celebrated. Many honor the courageous suffragists who fought tirelessly to ensure that women's voices would start to be heard in a concrete way. Yet, as **former ABA President Paulette Brown** and the **Honorable Lisa Atkinson** discuss in their respective essays on trailblazing women of color and Native women in the United States, others view this moment in our country's history as a time when society and the law did not go far enough to ensure that all women would be included. Other agendas won out, and significant portions of our country's population, notably women of color and Native women, remained excluded from the right to exercise their voices due to discriminatory policies and other obstacles.

Why are voting rights such an important issue? The right to vote sends a clear message of belonging to a society and empowering its members to be active participants in the direction and representation of their government. Any barrier impeding this fundamental right sends a message of not belonging, not being valued, and, in essence, not being worthy of representation. As individuals, casting our vote represents that singular moment when we can express our views and our priorities for what we want our life and our society to look like without judgment or reservation. Whether we choose to be public about whom we cast our vote for is our choice, but irrespective of whether or how we may decide to share our political views, by voting, we have the opportunity to shape our future and to choose individuals whose views we feel most closely represent who we are and what we want for our future. Casting a vote is an expression of power, an expression of inclusion, and a formal statement of participation in society. Short of holding an elected office ourselves, there is nothing more powerful than that. And that makes it worth continuing the fight for equality in women's voting rights, shining a light on the continued inequities, and identifying how we can all play a role in leveling the playing field to give men and women alike of every race, color, gender, religion, and socio-economic standing an equal voice.

The challenges to achieving gender equality in voting are not reserved to the United States. Technically speaking, aside from Vatican

City, women legally have the right to vote in every country around the world. But we know the reality is that, in many jurisdictions, the struggles are shared experiences around the world. Women remain disenfranchised from polling places, political parties, elected office, and public policy decision-making. Many experiences are similar to those we find in the United States. Others we would find unimaginable. While constitutional provisions and legislation have effectuated great strides around the world to grant women the right to vote and bring us closer to gender equality, these disparate experiences beg the question of how women's full voting rights and political inclusion can be effectively achieved and entrenched in our varied societies.

Women's economic empowerment and physical security are some of the major factors for advancing women's ability to exercise their right to vote. In her essay about elections and women's political rights in Kenya, **Rachel Irura** shares her firsthand experience with election-related violence and the barriers and risks faced by rural women. Her essay depicts life-threatening dangers that many would not think to connect with women exercising their right to vote. She explores why societal changes must also occur for women's voices to truly be heard and for women to be able to participate in society in accordance with their legal right to do so.

Voting rights are only one component of women's political participation. Women must also be empowered to vote for candidates of their choice, run as candidates, serve in elected offices, and exercise their voices within the political sphere. In many of the essays, the authors provide insights on strategies and approaches used in their countries for overcoming obstacles and for expanding women's political enfranchisement.

Shima Rostami, for example, describes in her essay how a series of Iranian feminist movements aimed at broadening women's role in society eventually led to women's right to vote. Yet, women felt their right to vote and other legal rights were ineffective and unequal to men without meaningful inclusion in political decision-making and society. She reflects on the similarity of Iranian women's experiences with women's movements in different parts of the world and the continued need for a global movement to end all forms of discrimination against women.

Taking an evidence-based and data-driven look at the experiences in Latin America and the Caribbean, **Alejandra Mora Mora** describes how gender quotas have elevated countries in the region to become global leaders in women's participation in legislatures. She identifies important factors in the effective design, implementation, and enforcement of gender quotas. As she notes, however, these affirmative measures to correct imbalances are not intended as permanent solutions. Her essay highlights how broader societal, political, and legal changes are essential for including women in all their diversity and in all aspects of life. Without those significant changes, true parity can never be accomplished.

Practical experiences of advancing women's rights in Brazil, in particular, show an evolution of women's constitutional and legal rights and harmonization with the treaty-based obligations of CEDAW. In her essay, **Carla Amaral de Andrade Junqueira** describes the implementation of legislative reforms, gender quotas, gender-responsive policies, and specialized institutions focused on women's issues. She explores how, despite these achievements, gender gaps remain for women's full inclusion in decision-making roles in government, diplomacy, and the workforce and provides recommendations for closing those gaps.

In Guatemala, women historically lagged in political participation, despite having had the legal right to vote. In recent years, however, women are increasingly participating as registered voters, candidates, and elected legislators. **María Isabel Luján Zilbermann** and **Fernanda Monzón Arroyo** discuss how improvements in government identification systems, registries, and electoral processes are driving these trends. They also discuss a range of persistent barriers, particularly for rural and Indigenous women, the growth in online and off-line harassment targeting women politicians, and possible approaches for future action to address those obstacles and promote further progress.

In their essay on the electoral landscape and political glass ceilings in India, the world's largest democracy, **Arya Tripathy** and **Priti Suri** address women's political participation within broader political, social, and cultural contexts. They share insights on how women's rights advocates are making progress with advancing gender parity and gender-responsive policies. They identify specific actions that government, political parties, legislatures, and advocates can take to advance closing the gender gap in politics and, more broadly, in society.

Australia was on the forefront of women's suffrage, extending voting rights to women in 1902, nearly two decades before the 19th Amendment. Yet, the right to vote did not herald the full or universal participation by women in elections and political life, as discussed by the **Honorable Margaret Beazley, AC, KC,** and **Elizabeth Chapman**. Their essay demonstrates how steps toward enfranchisement for women, including Indigenous women, evolved and must be understood in the contexts of constitutional interpretation, legislative actions, hard-fought legal battles, and underlying societal shifts. They discuss approaches for closing remaining gender gaps not only in political participation and power but also in every dimension of life, with voting being a critical right for accessing women's full range of rights.

Across the essays, we see these similar themes reinforced. Women can develop their fullest potential only when their rights are respected. While some of the issues of achieving gender equality and women's political empowerment may differ in certain respects or be more pronounced in certain parts of the world, on the whole, women must be able to realize the full range of their rights free from discrimination, prejudice, poverty, and harassment. Having the right to vote and ability to run for and hold office are essential to women's meaningful participation in society; however, societal, cultural, socio-economic, religious, and other factors are similarly powerful and influential forces over women's ability to gain true equality.

In her essay on women's political rights in Japan, **Hayashi Yoko** stresses the importance of pushing back against modern-day threats to women's rights domestically and worldwide: "We have not just an opportunity but also an obligation to overcome historical inequities and discrimination and to infuse our future with inclusion, diversity, and equality."

Now is a time for action, says **Christina Blacklaws**, in her essay on women's right to vote and women's inclusion in the legal profession in the United Kingdom. She offers specific calls to action informed by research surveys of lawyers, women and men, around the world. These recommendations apply to advancing gender equality and inclusiveness in the legal field and include themes related to the unique challenges faced by women of color and women who have disabilities.

The accounts reflected in this book are both a celebration of the progress women, men, and many societies around the world have made with regard to women's rights and voter equality and a testament to the importance and magnitude of the work that remains. More than anything, though, they speak to the power of women's voices and underscore the need for women around the world to have the ability to utilize that power to contribute to the shaping of a society they wish for themselves, their families, their communities, and generations to come.

My hope is that, after you have read each of these essays, you will have a greater understanding of where our global society currently sits on the spectrum of gender equality in voting, the issues still being faced, and the work that remains to be done for women to realize their full and equal political participation, and will feel inspired to play a role in achieving gender equality and women's full inclusion in all aspects of life.

1

The Americas: Advances, Persistent Obstacles, and New Challenges

Alejandra Mora Mora[1]

In the context of the 100th anniversary of women's suffrage in the United States in 2020, this chapter analyzes the progress in the substantive exercise of women's political rights in the Americas region, as well as the persistent obstacles and new challenges that arise in terms of women's access to and permanence in spaces of power. The Americas are the global leaders in the representation of women in legislatures, with a regional average of 32.4 percent,[2] and the experience of several countries with the effective implementation of parity can serve as a model for the rest of the region. In this context, the work of the Inter-American Commission of Women (CIM) of the Organization of American States (OAS) seeks to promote and advance parity and women's leadership in political life as a sine qua non for the strengthening and legitimacy of democratic governance.

Regional Legal and Policy Frameworks

The legal and policy framework surrounding the political rights of women in the Americas is solid and provides essential support to the full exercise of their citizenship. This framework includes international legal

1. Alejandra Mora Mora is the Executive Secretary of the Inter-American Commission of Women (CIM) of the Organization of American States (OAS). The views expressed are the author's personal views.

2. *Global and Regional Averages of Women in National Parliaments*, Inter-Parliamentary Union, https://data.ipu.org/women-averages (last updated June 1, 2021).

instruments, such as the American Declaration of the Rights and Duties of Man (American Declaration),[3] the International Covenant on Civil and Political Rights (ICCPR)[4] and the Convention on the Elimination of All Forms of Discrimination Against Women (CEDAW);[5] regional instruments, such as the Inter-American Conventions on the Granting of Civil and Political Rights to Women;[6] and political agreements, such as the Beijing Declaration and Platform for Action,[7] the Inter-American Program on the Promotion of Women's Human Rights and Gender Equity and Equality (IAP),[8] and the Inter-American Democratic Charter.[9]

Article 7 of CEDAW has been the starting point for the universal guarantee and protection of women's political rights since its entry into force in 1981:

> States Parties shall take all appropriate measures to eliminate discrimination against women in the political and public life of the country and, in particular, shall ensure to women, on equal terms with men, the right:
>
> a. To vote in all elections and public referenda and to be eligible for election to all publicly elected bodies;
> b. To participate in the formulation of government policy and the implementation thereof and to hold public office and perform all public functions at all levels of government;

---

3. American Declaration of the Rights and Duties of Man, Res. XXX, Final Act of the Ninth International Conference of American States (Pan American Union), Bogota, Colombia, Mar. 30–May 2, 1948, at 38.

4. International Covenant on Civil and Political Rights, Dec. 16, 1966, 999 U.N.T.S. 171.

5. Convention on the Elimination of All Forms of Discrimination Against Women, Dec. 18, 1979, 1249 U.N.T.S. 13.

6. Organization of American States (OAS), Inter-American Convention on the Granting of Civil Rights to Women, May 2, 1948, O.A.S.T.S. No. 38, 1438 U.N.T.S. 51; OAS, Inter-American Convention on the Granting of Political Rights to Women, May 2, 1948, O.A.S.T.S. No. 3, 1438 U.N.T.S. 63.

7. Beijing Declaration and Platform for Action, U.N. Doc. A/CONF. 1 77/20 (1995).

8. Inter-American Program on the Promotion of Women's Human Rights and Gender Equity and Equality, OAS Doc. OEA/Ser.P/AG/Res.1732 (2000); 30th Sess., OAS Doc. OEA/Ser.P/AG/Res.1732 (XXX-O/00) (OAS General Assembly) (June 5, 2000) (original in Spanish).

9. Inter-American Democratic Charter, OAS Doc. OEA/Ser.P/AG/Res. 1 (2001); 28th Spec. Sess., OAS Doc. OEA/Ser.P/AG/Res.1 (XXVIII-E/O1) (OAS General Assembly) (Sept. 11, 2001), 40 I.L.M. 1289 (2001).

c. To participate in non-governmental organizations and associations concerned with the public and political life of the country.[10]

This legal framework has been strengthened with the adoption of other instruments and agreements that address the multiple challenges to the full participation and leadership of women, such as the Inter-American Convention on the Prevention, Punishment, and Eradication of Violence Against Women (1994) (Belém do Pará Convention).[11] Article 4, paragraph j, of the Belém do Pará Convention reiterates the right of women to ". . . have equal access to the public service of her country and to take part in the conduct of public affairs, including decision-making."[12]

Women's Rights in a Patriarchal System: The Rules of the Game

This legal and policy framework was adopted and is being implemented within patriarchal systems, where the rules of the game do not yet favor women. Democratic structures, institutions, and processes are androcentric, designed by men, and continue to favor men in the exercise of power, both in the public and private spheres.

Inequality between women and men is a structural reality in our societies that affects the participation and incidence of women not only in the political sphere but also in all spheres of life. Two realities, in particular, structure the exercise of women's political-electoral rights in all the countries of the region: the feminization of poverty and the sexual division of labor.

Women still have a lower relative rate of participation in employment, lower average income under similar conditions of occupation and education, a higher incidence of unemployment, and greater participation in different forms of job insecurity, such as unregistered salaried jobs, low-productivity self-employment, and part-time jobs, among others. They also have less access to credit and other financial resources, property and landownership, inheritance, and natural resources, such as

10. *See* Convention on the Elimination of All Forms of Discrimination Against Women art. 7, Dec. 18, 1979, 1249 U.N.T.S. 13 (entered into force Sept. 3, 1981).

11. *See* OAS, Inter-American Convention on the Prevention, Punishment, and Eradication of Violence Against Women, June 9, 1994, 1438 U.N.T.S. 63 [hereinafter Belém do Pará Convention], http://www.oas.org/es/mesecvi/convencion.asp.

12. *Id.* art. 4(j).

energy and water. Further, women participate less in decision-making spaces and policy formulation in the economic field.

Parallel and causally, women continue to carry the burden of unpaid work, particularly unpaid care work, which is a common pattern across all the countries of the region. This historical sexual division of labor continues to be the main obstacle, along with gender-based violence, to the full and equal participation of women in all spheres of life.

The result is that women are poorer than men, and they do not derive the same benefits, including the same economic autonomy or independence as men, from their participation in productive employment. This situation, which includes time poverty and less access to all the resources necessary for political activity, has decisive implications for women's political participation.

In this context of power asymmetries, in the Americas, we are experiencing a profound democratic crisis that has its roots in inequality, the concentration of power and wealth, and the inability of people to realize their basic rights and to ensure the survival and development of their families. Democracy does not respond to the demands of the people, 50 percent of whom are women, and lacks representativeness and transparency in the face of equality gaps that are widening and deepening.

Finally, in recent years, we have seen the growth of a backlash against women's rights and gender equality with the arrival of mainstream currents of thought, speech, social movements, and even political parties that have as fundamental principles the inferiority and subordination of women and the rejection of sexual and gender diversity.[13] The financial and political power of these movements represents a real and significant threat to advances in women's rights and in particular their presence, incidence, and leadership in the public sphere.

Women's Suffrage and the Inter-American Commission of Women (CIM)

The Inter-American Commission of Women (CIM) was born at the beginning of the 20th century when women's suffrage movements were finally beginning to see concrete results. In 1922, the Pan American Association for the Advancement of Women was founded to influence

13. *See* OAS, Inter-American Comm'n of Women (CIM), *Inter-American Guidelines on Gender Equality for the Good of Humanity* 9–12 (2017), http://www.oas.org/en/CIM/docs/LineamientosIgualdadGeneroBien-EN.pdf.

the Fifth International Conference of American States (the forerunner to the establishment of the OAS in 1948), particularly from the perspective of the legal status of women and their right to vote. In this sense, "unofficial" delegates came to the conferences to lobby for women's suffrage.

The CIM was established during the Sixth International Conference of American States (Havana) as a result of coordinated work between women from the United States and Latin America. A group of prominent U.S. suffragists, including Alice Paul and Doris Stevens, led the negotiation for the adoption of the Equal Rights Treaty that would have raised the consideration of women's political rights to political debates throughout the hemisphere. However, the official representatives of the 21 countries present at the Sixth Conference insisted that only they had the right to speak, and that the meeting's agenda had no room for discussion of an equal rights treaty.[14]

Although the Equal Rights Treaty was not ratified, the decision was made to create the CIM. The creation of the CIM was a product of nascent women's movements across the hemisphere and reflected increased cooperation among women in North, Central, and South America. In her first speech to the conference in 1928, the first president of the CIM, Doris Stevens (United States), together with other feminist leaders, used the notion of Pan-Americanism to emphasize ". . . the necessity of action through the Pan American Conference, not by separate countries, in obtaining equal rights for women in all the American republics."[15]

Despite the fact that the Equal Rights Treaty for women had not been adopted, the CIM promoted a series of legal tools for the recognition and guarantee of women's rights and, in 1948, joined the OAS as an autonomous body with its own authorities. Every three years, CIM is responsible for organizing its Assembly of Delegates to discuss key issues of concern to women of the Americas and to prepare recommendations for other ministerial and high-level meetings, including the Summit of the Americas. The CIM is the first forum to generate hemispheric policies that seek to close the gap between the international legal framework on human rights and gender equality and public policy at the national level.

---

14. *See* OAS, CIM, A Brief History of the Inter-American Commission of Women (2018), http://www.oas.org/en/cim/docs/BriefHistory[EN].pdf.
15. *Id.* at 2–3.

The Situation Today: Progress and Persistent Obstacles

In the Americas region, much progress has been made in the participation, representation, and political leadership of women. In fact, the Americas are the global leader in terms of women's representation in legislatures, with a regional average of 32.4 percent, although that average hides significant variation across countries (see Table 1), from Bolivia with 46.2 percent in the lower house and 55.6 percent in the upper house to Belize with 12.5 percent in the lower house and 35.7 percent in the upper house.[16]

Table 1: Representation of Women in World Legislatures by Region

	Combined	Lower house	Upper house
Americas	32.4%	32.3%	33.0%
Europe	30.4%	30.5%	30.2%
Sub-Saharan Africa	25.2%	25.4%	24.5%
Asia	20.5%	21.0%	17.8%
Middle East/North Africa	17.9%	19.5%	11.2%
Pacific	21.5%	18.6%	44.9%

Source: Inter-Parliamentary Union[17]

In terms of other powers, data from the United Nations Economic Commission for Latin America and the Caribbean (ECLAC) indicates that, in Latin America, women make up 28.5 percent of executive cabinets,[18] 15.5 percent of mayors,[19] and 29.6 percent of city councilors.[20] Data from the International Institute for Democracy and Electoral Assistance (International IDEA) and the Inter-American Development Bank (IDB) indicates that gender inequities persist in political parties

16. *Monthly Ranking of Women in National Parliaments*, Inter-Parliamentary Union, https://data.ipu.org/women-ranking (last updated June 1, 2021).

17. *Global and Regional Averages of Women in National Parliaments*, *supra* note 2.

18. *Executive Power: Percentage of Women in Ministerial Cabinet Positions*, U.N., Econ. Comm'n for Latin Am. & the Caribbean [ECLAC], https://oig.cepal.org/en/indicators/executive-power-percentage-women-ministerial-cabinet-positions (last visited June 21, 2021).

19. *Elected Mayors Who Are Female*, ECLAC, https://oig.cepal.org/en/indicators/elected-mayors-who-are-female (last visited June 21, 2021).

20. *Elected City Council Members Who Are Female*, ECLAC, https://oig.cepal.org/en/indicators/elected-city-council-members-who-are-female (last visited June 21, 2021).

in selected countries in Latin America. Their studies between 2009 and 2015 showed that although women represented more than 50 percent of the membership of political parties, they made up 20 percent or less of the leadership in certain countries.[21]

Without a doubt, the advance that has had the most impact in recent years is **parity**. According to the CIM's definition, parity is a measure of justice that touches on three dimensions: (1) equal participation of women and men (50/50) in decision-making positions in the public and private sectors, from the international level to the local level; (2) exercise of power under conditions of equality, that is, free from discrimination and violence based on gender and/or sex; and (3) the incorporation of the agenda for women's rights and gender equality. Starting in 2009, a growing number of countries in Latin America have adopted parity as a way to deepen and consolidate the progress made with their quota laws.

Quota laws, adopted in 16 countries in the region between 1991 and 2015, seek to correct the existing asymmetry between women and men in access to elected office, based on the persistence of discrimination and the absence of women from democratic institutions. In general, quota laws are compensatory and redistributive measures conceptualized as temporary and necessary to correct an imbalance, but not permanent. Quota laws had highly differential impacts in the countries where they were adopted, however, due to a variety of factors. These include deficiencies in the normative design of the laws, such as the absence of the position mandate, their nonmandatory nature, the absence of sanctions for noncompliance, and random percentages between 20 percent and 45 percent that do not correspond to women's distribution in society or political parties.

Similarly, a country's political culture has been a determining factor in the effective application of quota laws. In several countries, maneuvers have been made to circumvent or avoid the law, such as the concentration of women in late candidacy positions or in losing districts. In others, the participation of women in electoral lists has been tied to arbitrary criteria

21. Int'l IDEA & Inter-Am. Dev. Bank [IDB], Partidos Políticos y Paridad: Una Mirada Subregional a América Central, República Dominicana y México [Gender and Political Parties: A Subregional Look at Central America, the Dominican Republic, and Mexico] 11–12 (Dec. 31, 2015) (Spanish), https://www.idea.int/sites/default/files/publications/partidos-politicos-y-paridad.pdf; Int'l IDEA & IDB, Mujeres y Partidos Políticos: La Ecuación Pendiente [Gender and Political Parties: Far from Parity] 30 (2011) (English, Spanish), https://www.idea.int/publications/catalogue/partidos-politicos-y-paridad-la-ecuacion-pendiente.

such as having to undergo prior training. Finally, in many countries, there continues to be a stereotypical vision of women's political participation as an "experience," instead of the vision of men who participate to "build a political career."

The characteristics of the electoral system are also an important factor in the effective implementation of quota laws, including the types of lists, the size of electoral districts, and the capacity of the national electoral institution and court to demand and justify implementation.

In other countries, over time, quota laws became more effective, and eventually the established percentages came to be seen as a ceiling rather than a floor, limiting women's representation to far below true equality. Hence, a number of countries went on to adopt parity. Parity represents a paradigm shift in terms of how we understand the concept of equality in political representation, and its effective implementation requires a social reordering in terms of shared responsibilities in both the public and private-domestic spheres. Parity assumes that political power must be shared between women and men as a premise of the universal human condition, justified in a balanced demographic presence: 50 percent women and 50 percent men (see Table 2).

Table 2: Quotas and Parity: Conceptual Differences

	Gender quotas	Gender parity
Objective	Correct	Transform
Strategy	Accelerate	Balance
Procedure	• Random percentages: 20%–45% • Not all regulations include a position mandate or punishment for noncompliance	• Equitable percentage: 50%–50% • Position mandate: alternation and sequence • Noncompliance carries a punishment
Duration	Temporary	Definitive/permanent
Scope	Limited	Broad

Source: UN Women[22]

22. Inés Tula, U.N. Women, Colección de Documentos Guía para Poderes Públicos y Tomadores de Decisión en América Latina y el Caribe: Paridad de Género, Política e Instituciones: Hacia una Democracia Paritaria [Collection of Guiding Documents for Public Authorities and Decision-Makers in Latin America and the Caribbean: Gender Parity: Politics and Institutions: Towards Democratic Parity] 1–30 (2018) (Spanish), http://lac.unwomen.org/es/digiteca/publicaciones/2018/2/paridad-de-genero-politica-e-instituciones.

Effectively, parity has made possible the constitution of equal, or nearly equal, parliaments for the first time in the history of the region. The common characteristic of these norms is the adoption of parity in the electoral sphere, although Mexico and Chile recently made a qualitative leap forward on this path. The 2019 constitutional reform instituted in Mexico, coined by Mexican feminists as "Parity Everywhere" [*Paridad en Todo*], entails the extension of parity to all state institutions. Chile, within the framework of elections to the Constituent Assembly that will draft a new constitution, applied a so-called parity by result, going beyond parity in electoral candidacies to a final tally of 49.3 percent of seats for women in the new assembly. The social demand for parity was a central aspect in the public debate regarding the composition of the constituent assembly in Chile and has placed the country on the path to the first constitution in the world that will emanate from a fully representative body.

Parity has served to resolve the heterogeneity seen in the design and implementation of quota laws, with more consistent results over time in all the countries that have adopted it (see Table 3). These eight countries—Argentina, Bolivia, Costa Rica, Ecuador, Honduras, Mexico, Nicaragua, and Peru—are now among the 30 countries in the world with the highest representation of women in their legislatures. In operational terms, parity implies that candidacies for popularly elected positions include an equal number of women and men (50/50). Similarly, two ordering criteria ensure the effective implementation of parity: vertical and horizontal parity. *Vertical parity* is the obligation of political parties to integrate women in half of their lists for the various types of elected office. *Horizontal parity* applies to the position of women in electoral lists across levels (national, state/provincial, municipal, etc.),[23] in addition to mechanisms for heading lists and braided lists that increase the chances of women being elected on equal terms with men. It should be noted that another mechanism to guarantee parity, as well as quota laws, has been the existence of a punishment for noncompliance.

---

23. U.N. Women, La Hora de la Igualdad Sustantiva. Participación Política de las Mujeres en América Latina y el Caribe Hispano [The Time for Substantive Equality: Political Participation of Women in Latin America and the Hispanic Caribbean] (2015) (Spanish), https://lac.unwomen.org/es/digiteca/publicaciones/2015/09/la-hora-de-la-igualdad.

Table 3: Quotas and Parity: Results in the Americas

Gender quotas	Percentage: Target	Percentage: Actual in lower chamber	Gender parity	Percentage in lower chamber
Paraguay	20%	15.0%	Bolivia	46.2%
Brazil	30%	15.2%	Mexico	48.2%
Guyana	30%	35.7%	Nicaragua	47.3%
Uruguay	33%	24.2%	Costa Rica	45.6%
Colombia	30%	18.8%	Argentina	42.4%
Haiti	30%	--	Peru	40.0%
El Salvador	30%	27.4%	Ecuador	38.0%
Dominican Republic	40–60%	27.9%	Panama*	22.5%
Chile	40–60%	22.6%	Honduras**	21.1%

Source: UN Women,[24] Inter-Parliamentary Union,[25] and National Office for Electoral Processes of Peru/ONPE[26]

* In Panama, parity is required in political parties only in relation to the selection of their candidacies and not in their presentation in elections. In 2017, parity was established without a position mandate, but with a penalty for noncompliance, with an exception to the mandatory requirement if the number of women in the selection process is less than 50 percent.

** In 2017, Honduras adopted the "Regulation to apply the principle of parity and the mechanism of alternation in the political participation of women and men in electoral processes," but it was invalidated by a resolution of the Supreme Electoral Tribunal. The promulgation of a new Electoral Law in 2019 voids that resolution.

Quotas and parity have been the most important reforms aimed at promoting women's political rights in the Americas.[27] Their positive effects have been both quantitative, in terms of the rapid increase in women's access to elected office (see Table 3), and qualitative, in terms of greater visibility of women in positions of power and the normalization of their participation outside the private sphere.

Based on this experience, the CIM, together with other organizations, has made concrete recommendations on the implementation of quota

24. *Id.* at Table 1.

25. *Monthly Ranking of Women in National Parliaments*, *supra* note 15.

26. *Results: 2021 General Elections*, ONPE PERU (NATIONAL OFFICE FOR ELECTORAL PROCESSES), https://www.onpe.gob.pe/modElecciones/elecciones/2021/EEGG/ (last visited Aug. 2, 2021).

27. For further information about the adoption and impact of parity, see CIM & INT'L IDEA, LE DEMOCRACIA PARITARIA EN AMÉRICA LATINA: LOS CASOS DE MÉXICO Y NICARAGUA [DEMOCRATIC PARITY IN LATIN AMERICA: THE CASES OF MEXICO AND NICARAGUA] (2016) (Spanish), http://www.oas.org/en/cim/docs/DemocraciaParitaria-MexNic-ES.pdf; INT'L IDEA & CIM, LA APUESTA POR LA PARIDAD: DEMOCRATIZANDO EL SISTEMA POLITICO EN AMÉRICA LATINA: LOS CASOS DE ECUADOR, BOLIVIA Y COSTA RICA [BANKING ON PARITY: DEMOCRATIZING THE POLITICAL SYSTEM IN LATIN AMERICA: THE CASES OF ECUADOR, BOLIVIA, AND COSTA RICA] (2013) (Spanish), http://www.oas.org/en/cim/docs/ApuestaPorLaParidad-Final-Web.pdf.

and parity laws. These include that the laws should be mandatory for all political parties, fronts, alliances, and other groups, so that progress does not remain subject to the goodwill of party leadership. Other priorities are the inclusion of the position mandate: vertical parity (in the heading of the lists) and horizontal parity (territorial); "gender substitution" mechanisms that ensure respect for the quota/parity in the replacement of candidates who resign; non-registration of electoral lists as a punishment for noncompliance; and a conducive electoral system, with large closed and blocked multi-member lists.

With some exceptions, parity has been applied mainly to the legislative branch and at the national level, leaving out other branches of government (executive, judicial, public administration, etc.), as well as the provincial/state, municipal, and regional/international levels (see Figure 1). The application of parity in other areas and in other branches is contemplated in some countries. In Bolivia in particular, parity is applicable in all branches and at all levels, although achieved with greater success in the legislative sphere at the national level.[28]

Equality in access to political office, however, is only part of the equation. In countries where this first goal has been achieved, women still report inequality in the exercise of power or in the conditions of

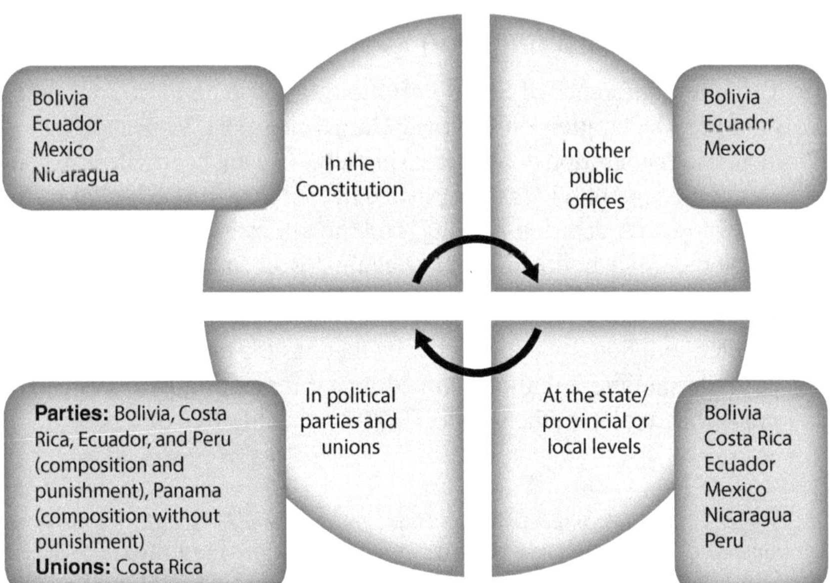

Figure 1: Toward Expanded Parity: First Advances of an Upcoming Agenda

28. *See* INT'L IDEA & CIM, *supra* note 26.

participation. In other words, they do not have the same levels of voice and influence, or the same decision-making power as men, even when they are present in relatively equal numbers.

This substantive approach to parity requires an examination of the many obstacles women still face in accessing positions of power and in exercising this power in conditions of equality and freedom from discrimination and violence. Similarly, the advance of parity and, in general, the agenda for gender equality have confronted deep-seated and, in some cases, growing resistance. In recent years, the unprecedented backlash against the advancement of women's rights in established democracies has been a source of grave concern. The anti-rights groups that are at the forefront of this backlash push an ultra-conservative agenda that questions the secular State and basic democratic principles[29] and contravenes the postulates of the Inter-American Democratic Charter and the link it establishes between democracy and human rights. As the participation of women progresses, there has been serious resistance to the advancement of parity and the increase in the presence of women in politics and political spaces. This backlash constitutes a form of gender-based violence against women that seeks to expel them from politics.

Violence Against Women in Political Life

In 2015, the Conference of States Party to the Belém do Pará Convention adopted the Declaration on Political Harassment and Violence Against Women,[30] in recognition of an increasing level of violence against women seeking to occupy public and, in particular, political spaces—that is, the exercise of power, decision-making, and the allocation of resources. The declaration defines political violence against women as:

> any action, conduct, or omission among others, based on their gender, individually or collectively, that has the purpose or result of undermining, annulling, impeding, or restricting their political rights, violating the rights of women to a life free of violence

29. *See* OAS, CIM, *Inter-American Guidelines on Gender Equality for the Good of Humanity* (2017), http://www.oas.org/es/cim/docs/LineamientosIgualdadGeneroBien-EN.pdf.

30. *See* OAS, Sixth Conf. of the States Parties to the Belém do Pará Convention, Lima, Peru, Oct. 15–16, 2015, *Declaration on Political Harassment and Violence Against Women*, OEA/Ser.L/II.7.10, MESECVI-VI/doc. 117/15.rev.2 (Oct. 15, 2015), https://www.oas.org/es/mesecvi/docs/DeclaracionViolenciaPolitica-EN.pdf.

and to participate in political and public affairs on an equal footing with men.[31]

Since then, in 2017, the Committee of Experts of the Follow-up Mechanism to the Belém do Pará Convention (MESECVI) adopted the Inter-American Model Law on the Prevention, Punishment and Eradication of Violence Against Women in Political Life,[32] which seeks to guide states in the formulation and effective implementation of legal/legislative instruments to confront political violence against women. Likewise, in 2019, the CIM published the Model Protocol for Political Parties: Preventing, Addressing, Punishing and Eradicating Violence Against Women in Political Life[33] to support the efforts of political parties in addressing this problem.

Other challenges faced by women include less access to electoral financing to launch and sustain their campaigns, the persistence of gender stereotypes in the media, and multiple discriminations based not only on the sex/gender of a candidate but also on their ethnicity, race, age, physical capacity, and sexual orientation, among other facets of their identity. In addition, women face the continued segregation of political functions by gender; they continue to predominate in "social" areas, such as health, education, social development, or culture, and not in areas such as defense/security, foreign policy, justice, economy/finance, and other areas that tend to have more power and more resources. Finally, the absence of concrete measures to promote co-responsibility between women and men in political spaces means that care will continue to be the main obstacle to the entry and permanence of women in these spaces.

New Challenges: COVID-19 and Women's Political Rights

While this chapter has been written in the context of the 100th anniversary of women's suffrage in the United States, it has also been written in an unprecedented historical context. A global health pandemic

31. *Id.* at 6.

32. *See* OAS, Inter-American Model Law on the Prevention, Punishment and Eradication of Violence Against Women in Political Life (2017), http://www.oas.org/en/mesecvi/docs/LeyModeloViolenciaPolitica-EN.pdf.

33. *See* OAS, CIM, Model Protocol for Political Parties: Preventing, Addressing, Punishing and Eradicating Violence Against Women in Political Life (2019), http://www.oas.org/en/cim/docs/ViolenciaPolitica-ProtocoloPartidos-EN.pdf.

and massive transnational mobilization for the human rights of afro-descendant people have put the question of power back on the table: who has it, how do they exercise it, and how are peoples' lives subject to that power. This questioning process makes it clear that, despite decades of activism and revindication, the exercise of power remains a question of White androcentrism.

The COVID-19 crisis presents particular challenges for women's rights. In its analysis of this situation, the CIM begins from the fact that the pandemic arises in a context of power asymmetries that are evident in multiple manifestations of discrimination and violence, which are deepened within the framework of COVID-19.[34] One of the most latent of these asymmetries is that, despite the fact that women have been and continue to be at the front lines of care and attention to the pandemic, their voices are almost imperceptible at the front lines of decision-making. Of all the ministries and secretariats for women in the Americas, in only two countries, namely Peru and Argentina, do they participate in the central committees or task forces established around the pandemic.

COVID-19 represents a huge risk of backsliding on the progress we have made on women's rights and gender equality. The exacerbation of existing inequalities is evident in an increase in economic inequalities that will deepen poverty and hunger among women and their families. Limitations and obstacles for women's participation in decision-making make them invisible in the design of public policies, social security systems, and all the responses to alleviate the economic crisis. Finally, gender-based violence has increased in almost all countries of the world because of confinement and social isolation/distancing measures.

In the framework of COVID-19, the CIM has established as an essential premise the equal participation of women in public decision-making. An examination of the participation of women in the management of previous pandemics (e.g., Zika virus in 2016, SARS in 2003) generates evidence of their importance and should condition the current context. It was clear when the crisis began that not considering a gender approach was going to deepen inequalities with effects that will last over the long term and will be difficult to reverse.

Nevertheless, multiple voices during the pandemic have sounded the alert over the limited participation of women in decision-making during the COVID-19 crisis. Turning this situation around and avoiding setbacks

34. *See* OAS, CIM, COVID-19 in Women's Lives: Reasons to Recognize the Differential Impacts, OEA/Ser.L/II.6.25 (2020), http://www.oas.org/en/cim/docs/ArgumentarioCOVID19-EN.pdf.

in terms of women's access to decision-making in the Americas must include a series of guarantees. First, the equal participation of women in decision-making is needed to offer effective and appropriate responses to the crisis from a gender perspective. Related to this is building the capacities of the National Machineries for the Advancement of Women to guarantee the gender and rights-based approach in the public policies of crisis management bodies.[35] An evaluation of the disproportionate impact of COVID-19 on the unpaid workload of women is essential to identifying the risks that this reality can pose for their effective participation in the political-electoral sphere. Governance with the participation of women and stressing the importance of concrete mechanisms will be essential to ensuring that electoral bodies and courts are prepared to ensure fairness in electoral campaigns and participation. Finally, the active participation of women in the evaluation and design of public policies and temporary measures to mitigate the crisis in all areas is a sine qua non for their effectiveness.

The red line is no setbacks in progress on women's rights in the region. The post-pandemic scenario requires first making women visible in all their diversity and from the intersectionality that allows us to understand how gender intersects with other facets of identity to deepen discrimination and marginalization. Then, it requires taking affirmative measures that balance differentiated impacts. Finally, we have to move from assessment and analyses to concrete policies and legal instruments that ensure nondiscrimination and the mitigation of violence, which will also help us to learn how states can respond in critical contexts and, at the same time, allow states to be better positioned against future global crises.

For all these measures to be effective, the participation and leadership of women are nonnegotiable. Without them, women's priorities and interests will remain invisible and will not be taken into account in decision-making and policy formulation to confront and mitigate the impacts of this global crisis.

Conclusions and a Look toward the Future

Although the Americas are in a time of deep uncertainty and insecurity, aggravated by the COVID-19 pandemic, the situation also presents us with new windows of opportunity to reclaim and advance the

35. *See id.* at 5, 8.

participation and leadership of women in public and, above all, in political spaces. Emerging evidence that women leaders have a different, innovative, and often more effective approach to all types of crisis combines with the normalization of the presence of women in spaces of power to present another possible reality, where the experiences and characteristics of women leaders as women contribute to creating fairer, more equitable, and peaceful societies.

From this vision, the CIM's strategic lines of work seek to promote parity by compiling and analyzing good practices in the region, strengthening the capacity of electoral institutions to protect and guarantee women's political rights, eradicate violence against women in political life, strengthen the capacity of women electoral candidates and other political women, and join the efforts of inter-American and international organizations to position women's political leadership as a priority on the inter-American agenda.

2

Australia: Citizenship, Participation, and Reality

The Honorable Margaret Beazley, AC, KC, and Elizabeth Chapman[1]

Australia was in the vanguard of women's suffrage, women being full voting participants in the federated Australian body politic from its inception. Australian leaders of the suffrage movement envisaged that the right to vote would carry with it full engagement in political decision-making and that with the right to vote would come true equality. This chapter investigates the extent to which that reality has, or has not, been achieved through the prism of the Australian Constitution and citizenship, and the extent to which other statutory reform has enabled and advanced equality. Our focus on women's suffrage is from a legal and experiential stance. In the Australian context, citizenship and participation in society have been largely coextensive for the male population.

Australian Constitution and Voting Rights

Australia became a federated commonwealth upon the commencement of the Constitution Act on January 1, 1901.[2] In the Constitutional Convention debates, which had taken place in the preceding decade, the framers of the constitution had taken guidance from the provisions of the U.S. Constitution. The outcome was that the general structure of the

1. The Honorable Margaret Beazley, AC, KC, is the 39th governor of New South Wales and former president of the New South Wales Court of Appeal, Australia. Elizabeth Chapman is a graduate lawyer and research assistant to the governor. She has a Bachelor of Art Theory/Arts (Hon.) and JD from the University of New South Wales (UNSW). The views expressed are the authors' personal views.

2. *Commonwealth of Australia Constitution Act 1901* (Imp), 63 & 64 Victoria, c. 12, § 9 (U.K.) [hereinafter AUSTRALIAN CONSTITUTION].

Australian Constitution has both similarities and differences with its U.S. counterpart,[3] particularly in respect of the doctrine of separation of powers and the separation of church and state. The separation of powers in Australia needs to be understood in the context of responsible government and the relationship between the executive and legislative branches. In relation to the separation of church and state, the High Court of Australia has taken a more narrow view of section 116, as compared with the interpretation of the 1st Amendment.

Notably absent from the Australian Constitution is any provision that entrenches the right to vote, although voting in Australia is compulsory.[4] A number of constitutional challenges to legislation have attempted to restrict the voting rights of certain segments of the community,[5] including challenges to compulsory voting,[6] electoral boundaries,[7] voting age,[8] and other restrictions on registering to vote.[9]

Those challenges aside, in Australia, there has been little juridical discussion as to what it *means* to have the right to vote. Nor has there been much academic or popular discussion as to the synergy between the right to vote and citizenship. While Australia has implemented international norms of equality in federal and state legislation,[10] for a society that proclaims itself as a modern democracy, built on notions of equality, and, indeed, a "fair go for all," strangely, it sits low on the scale of international metrics of women's participation in the society of which

3. *See* U.S. CONST.

4. The provision requiring compulsory voting was enacted in 1924. Currently in force is the *Commonwealth Electoral Act 1918* (Cth) s 245.

5. *See, e.g.*, *Roach v Electoral Comm'r* (2007) 233 CLR 162; *McGinty v W. Austl.* (1996) 186 CLR 140; *R v Pearson*; *Ex parte* Sipka (1983) 152 CLR 254.

6. *See Langer v Commonwealth* (1996) 186 CLR 302; *Judd v McKeon* (1926) 38 CLR 380.

7. *See McGinty*, at A-G (Commonwealth); *Ex rel McKinlay v Commonwealth* (1975) 135 CLR 1.

8. *See King v Jones* (1972) 128 CLR 221.

9. *See Rowe v Elec. Comm'r* (2010) 243 CLR 1; *Roach*, at 162.

10. Australia became a party to the Convention on the Elimination of All Forms of Discrimination Against Women on July 28, 1983, enacting its international law responsibilities in the *Sex Discrimination Act 1984* (Cth), *Anti-Discrimination Act 1977* (NSW), *Anti-Discrimination Act 1991* (QLD), *Anti-Discrimination Act 1992* (NT), *Anti-Discrimination Act 1998* (TAS), *Discrimination Act 1991* (ACT), *Equal Opportunity Act 1984* (SA), *Equal Opportunity Act 1984* (WA), and *Equal Opportunity Act 1995* (VIC). *See* Convention on the Elimination of All Forms of Discrimination Against Women, Dec. 18, 1979, 1249 U.N.T.S. 13 (entered into force Sept. 3, 1981).

they comprise more than 50 percent.[11] For the authors, this has raised questions as to whether, in Australia, it was the right to vote itself or antidiscrimination and other legislation that has been the real progenitor of change.[12]

The campaign for the female vote preceded the federation of Australia, and, it follows, the Australian Constitution. It was met with varied success in the different Australian colonies. South Australia led the way, with legislation passed in 1894 by one vote,[13] followed by Western Australia passing a motion in favor of women's suffrage in 1899.[14] Not even the "monster petition" of the 260-meter-long parchment containing approximately 30,000 signatures, presented to the Parliament of Victoria in 1891, succeeded in persuading that colony's parliament that the time for change had arrived.[15] It took another 17 years and 19 private member bills for women in that state to achieve the right to vote in their state elections.[16]

With no express right to vote, the focus in the Australian Constitution is on representative government, whereby members of the House of Representatives are chosen directly by the people.[17] The qualifications necessary for persons to be entitled to vote was left to Parliament.[18] At the

---

11. *The Health of Australia's Females*, AUSTL. INST. OF HEALTH & WELFARE, https://www.aihw.gov.au/reports/men-women/female-health (last updated Dec. 10, 2019) (reporting that there were 12.6 million females or 51 percent of people in Australia in 2018); *see also* AUSTL. L. REFORM COMM'N, REPORT NO. 67, EQUALITY BEFORE THE LAW: JUSTICE FOR WOMEN (1994).

12. *See generally Commonwealth Electoral Franchise Act 1902* (Cth); *Sex Discrimination Act 1984* (Cth); *Anti-Discrimination Act 1977* (NSW); *Equal Opportunity Act 1984* (SA); *Equal Opportunity Act 1984* (WA); *Anti-Discrimination Act 1991* (Qld); *Discrimination Act 1991* (ACT); *Anti-Discrimination Act 1992* (NT); *Sex Discrimination Act 1994* (Tas); *Equal Opportunity Act 1995* (Vic). The *Women's Legal Status Act 1918* (NSW) enabled women to practice as lawyers in New South Wales, becoming the second state to do so after Victoria in 1905.

13. *See Constitution Amendment Act 1894* (SA) (changing "man" to "person" and thereby extending suffrage to women).

14. *See* Western Australia, Parliamentary Debates, Legislative Assembly, 1899; *Constitution Acts Amendment Act* (passed Dec. 16, 1899; effective on May 18, 1900, for women over 21 years, excluding Indigenous, Africans, and Asians unless they were substantial landowners).

15. *Historical Information: Women's Suffrage Petition*, PARLIAMENT OF VICTORIA, https://www.parliament.vic.gov.au/about/the-history-of-parliament/womens-suffrage-petition (last visited June 21, 2021).

16. *See id.*

17. AUSTRALIAN CONSTITUTION ss 7, 8, 24, 29, 30.

18. *Id.* ss 8, 24, 30.

federal level, female enfranchisement was recognized at the outset with the passage of the Commonwealth Franchise Act 1902. However, we specifically refrain from describing this legislation as introducing universal suffrage. Persons of unsound mind, attainted of treason or imprisoned for an offence punishable by imprisonment for one year or longer, and Indigenous peoples from "Asia, Africa or the Islands of the Pacific except New Zealand" were excluded, and the right of Indigenous Australians to vote was convoluted to say the least.[19] It needs to be said, however, that Australia was not alone in conferring voting rights that did not encompass universal suffrage.[20]

The Right to Vote

Notwithstanding the absence of an express constitutional right to vote, the Australian High Court has accepted that Australia's form of democracy, encapsulated in the constitutional notion of representative government, is such that, in the Australian Constitution, there is a constitutional protection of the right to vote.[21] In *Roach v. Electoral Commissioner*, Chief Justice Gleeson observed that the words of sections 7 and 24 of the Australian Constitution, "because of changed historical circumstances

19. The *Commonwealth Franchise Act 1902* (Cth) is no longer in force; its provisions are included within the *Commonwealth Electoral Act 1918* (Cth). The latter act retained the same eligibility criteria for voting entitlements as its predecessor. Eligibility to vote for Indigenous Australians had a somewhat complicated legislative history. For the purposes of this chapter, it is sufficient to note that by 1962, the franchise for Commonwealth elections extended to all Indigenous Australians. In line with the general population, voting became compulsory for Indigenous Australians pursuant to amendments to the *Commonwealth Electoral Act* in 1983.

20. The 19th Amendment to the U.S. Constitution guaranteed citizenship and enfranchisement as coextensive. However, it was only in the 1960s, when the U.S. Supreme Court's jurisprudence shifted to a view of voting as a fundamental right under the 14th Amendment, that something more akin to universal enfranchisement was installed. The Court applied strict scrutiny to laws restricting enfranchisement, resulting in the poll tax, durational residency requirements in excess of 50 days, property ownership, and tax payment requirements being invalidated, and literacy and other testing of voters viewed with greater suspicion. *See, e.g.*, Burns v. Forston, 410 U.S. 686 (1973); Marston v. Lewis, 410 U.S. 679 (1973); Dunn v. Blumstein, 405 U.S. 330 (1972); City of Phoenix v. Kolodziejski, 399 U.S. 204 (1970); Harper v. Virginia Bd. of Elections, 383 U.S. 663 (1966); Carrington v. Rash, 380 U.S. 89 (1965).

21. AUSTRALIAN CONSTITUTION ss 7, 24.

including legislative history, have come to be a constitutional protection of the right to vote."[22] The Chief Justice continued:

> Because the franchise is critical to representative government, and lies at the centre of our concept of participation in the life of the community, and of citizenship, disenfranchisement of any group of adult citizens on a basis that does not constitute a substantial reason for exclusion from such participation would not be consistent with choice by the people.[23]

In the earlier 1996 decision, *McGinty v. Western Australia*, Justice Gaudron, Australia's first female High Court judge, stated that the meaning of the words "*chosen by the people*" in the constitution would not permit electoral franchise to be denied "to women or to members of a racial minority or to be made subject to a property or educational qualification."[24]

Neither *McGinty* nor *Roach* involved female enfranchisement. *McGinty* involved a challenge by Labor Party leader Jim McGinty to the 1996 Western Australian state election results, on the ground of unequal electoral boundaries. The challenge failed, the High Court pointing out that aside from the minimum requirements for representative government in sections 7 and 24, "the form of representative government which we are to have is left to parliament."[25]

Given the absence of an express constitutional right to vote, Justice Gaudron's observation as to the inviolability of female and other minority enfranchisement remains significant dicta in respect of a protected right in a common law system where the principle of stare decisis operates. However, that principle is not inviolable, although there would be few right-minded citizens, one would expect, who would deny the force of her Honor's comment.

Roach involved a challenge to the Electoral and Referendum Amendment (Electoral Integrity and Other Measures) Act 2006 (Cth).[26] The original legislation excluded those serving three years or more from voting. The amending provision disqualified all persons serving custodial

---

22. *Roach*, at 174 [7] (citing *McKinlay* (1975) 135 CLR 1, 36 (McTiernan and Jacobs JJ): "the long established universal adult suffrage may now be recognised as fact"); *McGinty*, at 286–87 (Gummow J)).

23. *Roach*, at 174 [7] (Gleeson CJ).

24. *McGinty*, at 222 (Gaudron J); *cf. Langer*, at 342 (McHugh J).

25. *McGinty*, at 183 (Dawson J).

26. *Electoral and Referendum Amendment (Electoral Integrity and Other Measures) Act 2006* (Cth).

sentences from voting. This blanket disqualification offended long-established law that disqualification was only appropriate where "conviction for certain descriptions of offence evinced an incompatible culpability which rendered those electors unfit . . . to participate," and was thus declared unconstitutional.[27]

To constitutionally astute U.S. citizens, the absence of an express right to vote may seem a significant shortcoming in the Australia Constitution and perhaps more so in a jurisdiction lacking a federal Bill of Rights. However, the protections afforded by a constitution are not at the forefront of Australian thinking,[28] prompting academic Helen Irving to observe "most Australians . . . do not understand the importance of constitutions."[29]

As apparent from the approach in the passage just cited from *Roach*, enfranchisement is connected to notions of participation: participation per se in the life of the community and the participatory right of persons to engage in the political life of the body politic, more closely aligned with citizenship. The distinction is not without a difference. Citizenship, in the Australian conception, has been closely linked with the right to live in Australia, secure from deportation, which Irving identifies as "the firmest and in many respects, the most essential of all the 'rights' held by citizens."[30] As our exploration of the topic has revealed, it is not only the right to vote but also rights conferred by or protected under other

---

27. *Roach v Electoral Comm'r* (2007) 233 CLR 162 55–62, 90 (Gummow, Kirby, Crennan JJ). William Blackstone made reference to several statutes providing that any person convicted of perjury or subornation of perjury was not capable of voting in any election. WILLIAM BLACKSTONE, COMMENTARIES ON THE LAWS OF ENGLAND bk. 1, ch. 2, at 167 (1769). This legal stance was included in the Australian Constitutions Act 1842 (Imp) s 6, which stipulated "no person shall be entitled to vote at any such Election who shall have been attainted or convicted of any Treason, Felony, or infamous Offence within any Part of Her Majesty's Dominions, unless he shall have received a free Pardon, or one conditional on not leaving the Colony, for such Offence, or shall have undergone the sentence or Punishment to which he shall have been adjudged for such Offence."

28. *Cf.* AV DICEY, INTRODUCTION TO THE STUDY OF THE LAW OF THE CONSTITUTION 198–202 (Macmillan 1st ed. 1885, 10th ed. 1959); SIR W. IVOR JENNINGS, THE LAW AND THE CONSTITUTION 54 (Univ. of London Press 5th ed. 1959); Eric Barendt, *Dicey and Civil Liberties [1985] Public Law 596*, *in* GEORGE WILLIAMS ET AL., BLACKSHIELD AND WILLIAMS AUSTRALIAN CONSTITUTIONAL LAW AND THEORY: COMMENTARY AND MATERIALS 98–100 (Fed'n Press 5th ed. 2010).

29. Helen Irving, *Why Constitutions Matter to Women*, 20 THE SYDNEY PAPERS 172, 173 (2008).

30. HELEN IRVING, GENDER AND THE CONSTITUTION: EQUITY AND AGENCY IN COMPARATIVE CONSTITUTIONAL DESIGN 96 (Cambridge Univ. Press 1st ed. 2008).

legislation that has been a significant enabler of participation but not the cure-all for constraints on women's full participation in Australia's democratic society.

It might be asked why we are scrabbling around in this topic in the 21st century given that John Stuart Mill wrote in 1861:

> [T]he best form of government is that in which the sovereignty or supreme controlling power in the last resort is vested in the entire aggregate of the community. . . . The meaning of representative government is that the whole people, or some numerous portion of them, exercise through deputies periodically elected by themselves the ultimate controlling power . . . .[31]

According to Mill, equality of the right to vote and to stand for parliament was "a principle of perfect equality, admitting no power or privilege on the one side, nor disability on the other."[32] Mill advocated for women's rights, arguing that the subordination of women was not only "wrong in itself" but was "one of the chief hindrances to human improvement."[33] While we consider these observations to be self-evident, nearly half a century passed before legislators first heeded this unquestionable wisdom. In many countries, it took a century for female enfranchisement to be introduced.

It is at this point that we pause to ask: "What is the relevance in contemporary Australia of this most basic right, and, in particular, what did the right to vote achieve for women?" It certainly hasn't achieved full and equal participation in all aspects of the life of the community. We do see it, however, as the launch pad without which other advances would never have been achieved. Consider a discussion around a boardroom table if a woman board member did not have the right to vote. Her contribution would readily be demeaned by the comment: "What would you know? You can't even vote." The right to vote therefore is properly seen as the formal statement by a parliament or congress that a person with the right to vote is an equal participant in society. Without that formal recognition, antidiscrimination and other legislation[34] would not have had the same

31. John Stuart Mill, Considerations on Representative Government chs III, V (1861).

32. John Stuart Mill, The Subjection of Women ch 1 (1869).

33. *Id.*

34. *Sex Discrimination Act 1984* (Cth); *Anti-Discrimination Act 1977* (NSW); *Equal Opportunity Act 1977* (Vic); *Equal Opportunity Act 1984* (SA); *Equal Opportunity Act 1984* (WA); *Anti-Discrimination Act 1991* (Qld); *Discrimination Act 1991* (ACT); *Anti-Discrimination Act 1992* (NT); *Sex Discrimination Act 1994* (Tas).

positive impact on women's participation in society. In short, without the right to participate in the election of the lawmakers and, further, without the right to be a lawmaker, women's participation in society would be incomplete.

In Australia, the Sex Discrimination Act 1984 (Cth) and its state counterparts have given effect to the country's international law obligations in eradicating "any distinction, exclusion or restriction made on the basis of sex which has the effect or purpose of impairing or nullifying the recognition, enjoyment or exercise by women, irrespective of their marital status, on a basis of equality of men and women, of human and fundamental freedoms."[35]

Yet, substantive inequality remains a palpable feature of contemporary Australian society. This can be demonstrated in various ways. As lawyers, we naturally gravitate to the case law. We have also investigated international statistical studies that reveal the shortfall in women's full participatory engagement in community life.

Women's Educational and Professional Participation: The Case Law

For women, full educational and professional participation has, in significant respects, only come about after hard-fought legal battles. Two cases in the 1980s demonstrate this.

In *Wardley v. Ansett Transport Industries*, Deborah Wardley, a qualified pilot, challenged Ansett Airlines' refusal to employ her as being discriminatory on the basis of her sex.[36] Among other evidence was this letter from the general manager:

> [Ansett] . . . [has] adopted a policy of only employing men as pilots. This does not mean that women cannot be good pilots, but we are concerned with the provision of the safest and most efficient air service possible. In this regard, we feel that an all male pilot crew is safer than one in which the sexes are mixed.[37]

35. *Sex Discrimination Act 1984* (Cth) art. 1; Convention on the Elimination of All Forms of Discrimination Against Women art. 1, Dec. 18, 1979, 1249 U.N.T.S. 13 (entered into force Sept. 3, 1981).

36. *See Wardley v Ansett Transport Indus.* (1984) EOC 92-002 (arguing the dismissal violated the *Equal Opportunity Act 1977* (Vic) s 18).

37. *Id.* at 75,260.

The general manager considered Ms. Wardley to be "a very nice person, highly intelligent and undoubtedly a good pilot, but that is not quite what we are talking about."[38] Her claim having succeeded, Ansett Airlines was ordered to employ Ms. Wardley in their next intake of pilots. Ansett Airlines unsuccessfully appealed to the High Court on the basis of constitutional inconsistency between state and federal legislation.[39] In the meantime, Ms. Wardley had lost more than five years of her professional life with implications for her salary and promotion, to say nothing of the stress of litigation, about which much has been written in Australia.[40]

In *Leves v. Haines*, Melinda Leves and her twin brother, Rhys, were offered different electives at their respective single-sex schools.[41] Rhys was able to study industrial design, while Melinda was restricted to home economics subjects, a euphemism in the Australian context at the time for cooking and low-level sewing skills. The Education Department was found to have discriminated against Melinda. Even though the Education Department had, seven years earlier, urged schools to strive toward providing a nonsexist education for girls, the reality in practice was that "[g]irls [were] still presumed to want and to gain benefit from the education which contains a domestically oriented component, rather than a career oriented component."[42] The young Ms. Leves' legal journey, difficult enough for anyone, was not without the additional stress of technical points being taken and unsatisfactory compromises being offered. In particular, the state government defendant unsuccessfully challenged Ms. Leves' right to bring the proceedings.[43] The offered compromise involved her traveling some distance to another school to obtain the same educational opportunities as her brother, disrupting, among other things, her existing social connections.

Both of these cases reflect discriminatory conduct that impeded the employment or education opportunities of the respective applicants. Similar situations would be unlikely to arise today, but new issues always

38. *Id.*

39. *See Ansett Transport Indus. (Operations) Pty Ltd v Wardley* (1980) 142 CLR 237.

40. *See, e.g., White v Overland* (2004) FCA 1333, 4 (Allsop J); *Baulderstone Hornibrook Eng'g Pty Ltd v Gordian Runoff Ltd* [2008] NSWCA 243, 160 (Allsop P); *Aon Risk Services Australia Ltd v Australian Nat'l Univ.* [2009] NSW 27, 100–01 (Gummow, Hayne, Crennan, Kiefel, and Bell JJ).

41. *See Leves v Haines* (1986) EOC 92-167 (involving a complaint of sex discrimination under section 31A of the Anti-Discrimination Act 1977 (NSW)).

42. *Haines v Leves* (1986) EOC 92-192.

43. *See Haines v Leves & Another* (1987) 8 NSWLR 442.

emerge. For example, the need for women to maintain employment with flexible conditions has brought into play different considerations, and, in particular, raises questions as to the legal position of the employer to facilitate requests for flexible work conditions not part of usual employee arrangements.

In *Howe v. Qantas Airways Ltd*, Lindy Howe brought a claim for damages and ancillary relief, alleging her employer discriminated against her on the basis of her family responsibilities, sex, and pregnancy, and, further, that she was constructively dismissed by Qantas following her return to work after a period of maternity leave.[44] Ms. Howe brought these claims under the Human Rights and Equal Opportunity Commission Act 1986 (Cth) and the Sex Discrimination Act 1984 (Cth).[45] Ms. Howe was a long-haul customer service manager. When she informed her employer she was pregnant, she was required to take either unpaid maternity leave or seek a ground-based position at a substantially reduced salary, with no access to sick leave. Upon returning to work, part-time employment was unavailable at her level and salary rate, leaving her obliged to take a lower paid position as a flight attendant to access the flexible working arrangements that she sought.

Ms. Howe lost her claim of indirect sex discrimination. The presiding magistrate ruled that the employer had not constructively dismissed Ms. Howe or failed to respond to her requests on the grounds alleged. Rather, the court accepted that the employer was unable to accommodate her requests, either for part-time employment, as no positions were available at the time, or for flexible working conditions. Ms. Howe's request for a transfer to another position, which was granted, was not, the court found, a "demotion" and, therefore, did not constitute a constructive dismissal.[46] Rather, the court found the position to which Ms. Howe had asked to be transferred gave her the flexible working conditions she was seeking. Strictly, this unsatisfactory outcome speaks for itself, and it is doubtful there would be a similar outcome in 2021. However, it does demonstrate the obstacles that women continue to encounter across a variety of employment and educational circumstances that hinder their advancement and, relevantly, their ability to participate in society according to their wishes and abilities.

44. *Howe v Qantas Airways Ltd* (2004) FMCA 242.
45. *See Sex Discrimination Act 1984* (Cth) ss 5(2), 7(1), 14(2)(a), (3A).
46. *Howe*, at 131.

Women's Empowerment: Closing the Gaps

Thirty-six years after the enactment of the Sex Discrimination Act 1984, the World Economic Forum's Global Gender Gap Report 2020 ranks Australia 44th behind Bolivia, Jamaica, Poland, and Serbia.[47] Topping the scale are Iceland, Norway, Finland, Sweden, Nicaragua, and New Zealand. The four quadrants of inequality upon which countries are ranked are economic participation and opportunity (49th), educational attainment (1st), health and survival (82nd), and political empowerment (57th).[48]

As the score on educational attainment reveals, Australia's female participation in higher education is significant. Since 2007, females aged 25 to 29 are more likely than males to attain a bachelor's degree or higher.[49] In 2020, 48.3 percent of females and 36.1 percent of males aged 25 to 29 in Australia had attained a bachelor's degree or higher, and 86.5 percent of females compared to 84.7 percent of males aged 15 to 19 were currently studying for a qualification.[50]

The disparity between educational attainment and performance in the other three quadrants reveals a continuing entrenchment of cultural and business attitudes inhibiting women's full participation in all aspects of society. According to the Australian Bureau of Statistics, women undergraduates in 2020 were paid less in starting salaries than men in all but four fields of study.[51] The gender pay gap is particularly apparent in the salaries within those professions that have tended to have a predominantly female workforce. In 2018, the most common occupations for men with a bachelor's degree or above were accountancy and software programming.[52] Meanwhile, the two professions with the highest rates of

47. World Econ. Forum, Global Gender Gap Report 2020, at 9 (2020). The report and an interactive data platform are available at http://reports.weforum.org/global-gender-gap-report-2020/dataexplorer.

48. *Id.*

49. *Gender Indicators, Australia*, Austl. Bureau of Statistics, https://www.abs.gov.au/statistics/people/people-and-communities/gender-indicators-australia/latest-release (last updated Dec. 15, 2020) (providing data on females and males).

50. *Id.* at Education and Data Cube 5: Education—Participation and Education and Employment.

51. *Id.* (showing the largest difference in dentistry where women's starting salaries were $79,300 compared to $90,000 for men).

52. Press Release, Austl. Bureau of Statistics, Australians Pursuing Higher Education in Record Numbers (Oct. 23, 2017), https://www.abs.gov.au/AUSSTATS/abs@.nsf/mediareleasesbyReleaseDate/1533FE5A8541D66CCA2581BF00362D1D.

female graduate participation remain two of the least well remunerated—registered nurses and primary school teachers.[53]

Australian women earn on average AUD $242.20 per week less than men.[54] In 2021, there was a 13.4 percent difference in average earnings between men and women,[55] with the national pay gap lingering between 14 percent and 19 percent for the prior two decades.[56] Professional, scientific, and technical services occupations have the highest deviation of earnings between genders, at 24.4 percent, followed closely by financial and insurance services at 23.6 percent and health care and social assistance at 21.2 percent.[57] Financial disparity entrenches a woman's financial disadvantage over a lifetime, affecting her purchasing power and her ability to save, and resulting in lower superannuation (retirement) benefits.[58]

The position is further impacted by a continuing assumption of the female as the primary caregiver. In 2016, the Household, Income, and Labour Dynamics in Australia Survey revealed that working-age women spent 24.9 hours on paid employment and 20.4 hours on unpaid household

53. *Id.*

54. Press Release, Austl. Workplace Gender Equality Agency, The National Gender Pay Gap Drops to 13.4% (Feb. 25, 2021), https://www.wgea.gov.au/newsroom/the-national-gender-pay-gap-drops-to-13.4%25.

55. *Id.*

56. *Gender Equality in Australia—A Guide to Gender Equality in 2020*, Austl. Workplace Gender Equality Agency (Sept. 25, 2020), https://www.wgea.gov.au/newsroom/latest-news/gender-equality-in-australia-a-guide-to-gender-equality-in-2020.

57. *Factsheet Series: Australia's Gender Pay Gap Statistics*, Austl. Workplace Gender Equality Agency (Feb. 2021), https://www.wgea.gov.au/sites/default/files/documents/Gender_pay_gap_fact_sheet_Feb2020.pdf.

58. *See* Austl. Bureau of Statistics, *2020 Gender Indicators, Australia* (Dec. 15, 2020) (see Table 2, showing the median superannuation balance for 55–64 years in 2017–18 was $119,000 for women compared to $183,000 for men), https://www.abs.gov.au/statistics/people/people-and-communities/gender-indicators-australia/2020. *See generally* Bina Brown, *Opinion: Why There Could Be a Financially Vulnerable Woman in Your Family: Females over 50 Are the Fastest-Growing Group of People at Risk of Homelessness*, Austl. Fin. Rev. (Nov. 21, 2019, 11:04 AM), https://www.afr.com/wealth/personal-finance/why-there-could-be-a-financially-vulnerable-woman-in-your-family-20191120-p53che; Simon Kelly et al., *Women and Superannuation in the 21st Century: Poverty or Plenty*, *in* Soc. Policy Research Ctr., Univ. of New South Wales, Rep. No. 1/02, Competing Visions: Referred Proceedings of the National Social Policy Conference, Sydney, 4–6 July 2001, 223–47 (Tony Eardley & Bruce Bradbury eds., 2002), https://www.aspc.unsw.edu.au/sites/www.aspc.unsw.edu.au/files/uploads/files/002-NSPC01_RefereedProceedings.pdf.

work, on average per week.[59] Of those unpaid hours, 11.3 hours were spent directly caring for children or disabled or elderly relatives. By contrast, men spent 35.9 hours in paid employment and 13.3 hours on housework, with 5.4 of those spent caring for children or relatives.

Where do women stand, then, in 2021? Unfortunately, not on an equal footing as this brief statistical overview illustrates. But there is more. In Australia, misogyny and other poor treatment of women remains an occasional but disturbing feature of public life. Prime Minister Julia Gillard's "misogyny speech" in the Australian Parliament in 2012 has gone down in the annals of great speeches of the century.[60] It is sufficient to refer to one comment Gillard quoted in her speech, made by Tony Abbott, then leader of the opposition and later Prime Minister of Australia, who, in 2010, during a campaign against a proposed emissions trading scheme, said: "What the housewives of Australia need to understand as they do the ironing . . ." is that electricity prices would rise.[61]

Nor did the right to vote usher in full participation in the political life of the country. Women in Australia were eligible to stand for federal Parliament at least from 1902.[62] Yet, it was not until 1943 that Australia's first female representatives, Enid Lyons and Dorothy Tangney, were elected to the Commonwealth Parliament. Australia's 46th Commonwealth Parliament, running from July 2019 to July 2022, is comprised of 86 women and 141 men—women making up 31.1 percent of the House of Representatives and, for the first time, 51.3 percent of the Senate.[63]

Helen Irving points out that the rights to vote and to run for office have often been conflated with citizenship and full membership of the constitutional community—thus equipping women with formal equality. The actual level of female participation belies that observation. A political culture that affirms and facilitates participation, providing structures that support this affirmation is the necessary prerequisite to achieving

---

59. Roger Wilkins & Inga Lass, Melbourne Inst.: Applied Econ. & Soc. Research, Melbourne Univ., The Household, Income and Labour Dynamics in Australia Survey: Selected Findings from Waves 1 to 16, at 82–83 (2018), https://melbourneinstitute.unimelb.edu.au/__data/assets/pdf_file/0009/2874177/HILDA-report_Low-Res_10.10.18.pdf.

60. *See* Cth, Parliamentary Debates, House of Representatives, 9 Oct. 2012, 11581 (Prime Minister Julia Gillard).

61. *Id.*

62. *See Commonwealth Franchise Act 1902* (Cth).

63. Anna Hough & Lisa Richards, *Gender Composition of Australian Parliaments by Party: A Quick Guide*, Parliament of Austl. (Mar. 8, 2022), https://www.aph.gov.au/About_Parliament/Parliamentary_Departments/Parliamentary_Library/pubs/rp/rp2122/Quick_Guides/CompositionPartyGender (see Table 1).

gender parity in the political realm. Quotas are one method of achieving statistical equality in representation.[64] However, to date, Australia's political parties and institutions have not significantly engaged with quotas—or indeed with targets—as a structure or mechanism for maximizing parity in policy formation and lawmaking or for facilitating membership of the constitutional community. Rather, the focus of debate on this issue has too often resided in the dangers of deprioritizing merit and valuing tokenism.

Sexual harassment is known to be rife in some professions, including in the legal profession. Consensual sexual conduct is neither illegal nor necessarily inappropriate. However, the fallout from relationships that break down all too often derails the career of a female party, with her employment and reputational position compromised. It is well documented that nonconsensual sexual or harassing conduct has severe effects on women's wish to remain within professions. Women represent over 60 percent of senior associates and graduate lawyers in Australia—yet they only exceeded 30 percent of partners in law firms for the first time in 2020.[65] Women represent only 24 percent of the bar and 12.7 percent of those appointed senior counsel, with rates of appointment in 2020 for female applicants on average just 2.5 percent higher than their male colleagues.[66]

More gravely, domestic and family violence remains a central health and welfare issue for Australians. More than 2.2 million Australians have experienced physical and/or sexual violence from a partner, and 3.6 million experienced emotional abuse.[67] On average, women are more than eight times more likely to be victims than men: 1 in 6 women compared to 1 in 16 men having experienced physical or sexual violence by a current or previous partner since the age of 15.[68]

---

64. *See* IRVING, *supra* note 30, at 118 ("Around forty countries in the world have gender quotas in their constitutions.").

65. Hannah Wootton, *Female Law Partners Break the 30pc Barrier*, AUSTL. FIN. REV. (Dec. 10, 2020, 2:27 PM), https://www.afr.com/companies/professional-services/women-partners-break-through-30pc-barrier-20201130-p56j7u.

66. *Senior Counsel Statistics in 2020*, NEW SOUTH WALES BAR ASS'N INBRIEF (Sept. 30, 2019), https://inbrief.nswbar.asn.au/posts/08b347d11316f1372f3414b4c431404a/attachment/senior%20counsel%20stats%202020.pdf.

67. AUSTL. INST. OF HEALTH & WELFARE, PUB. NO. FDV 4, FAMILY, DOMESTIC AND SEXUAL VIOLENCE IN AUSTRALIA: CONTINUING THE NATIONAL STORY 2019—IN BRIEF 1 (2019), https://www.aihw.gov.au/getmedia/b180312b-27de-4cd9-b43e-16109e52f3d4/aihw-fdv4-FDSV-in-Australia-2019_in-brief.pdf.

68. *Id.* at 3.

Conclusion

In this short chapter, we have sought to demonstrate that, in Australia, the right to vote, a hallowed feature of a modern democracy, has neither achieved full equality for women nor brought about sufficient societal change to enable Australia to say: "We are an equal society." Underlying institutional power structures, hierarchical professions, attitudinal notions of a "woman's place," inflexible work arrangements, and salary differentials deny women equality in a society where this should be their birthright.

We have seen that legislative change has promoted equality and aided its implementation, none of which could have occurred without the seminal first step of enfranchisement. However, we have also seen that enfranchisement in itself, and other legislation that supports women's engagement in society, is insufficient to change cultural attitudes that dictate what a woman can do. There continue to be those who hold power, whether that be political, economic, or institutional power, who seek to impose their perceptions of the society into which women *must* fit rather than embracing a society in which men and women determine for themselves how and the extent to which they wish to participate.

We conclude by expressing agreement with Helen Irving in this respect, that full membership of a constitutional community requires participation in every dimension and layer of lawmaking—voting being the necessary structural underpinning, or "master key," to access all other democratic rights.[69]

69. IRVING, *supra* note 30, at 114.

3

Brazil: Impacts, Barriers, and Gender Equality

Carla Amaral de Andrade Junqueira[1]

Women in Brazil had voting rights in 1932 with the enactment of the Brazilian Electoral Code,[2] yet they did not have equal voting rights until 1945 when voting became compulsory for both men and women.[3] Before 1945, married women needed permission from their husbands to vote because the Civil Code required women to get authorization from their husbands or fathers for activities in the public sphere.[4]

Women's participation in political life has been slow to emerge. With the government's "technocratization" of the Brazilian economy in the 1960s and 1970s, women benefited from expanded access to education and the workforce.[5] By 1975, the number of women college students increased and contributed to the feminist movement.[6] Yet, the government and the military continued to enshrine traditional roles for women,

1. Carla Amaral de Andrade Junqueira is a founding partner with Carla Junqueira & Associadas—CJA Trade Law, a law firm in Brazil.

2. Decreto no. 21.076, de 24 de Fevereiro de 1932, DIÁRIO OFICIAL DA UNIÃO [D.O.U.] t.1: 3385 de 2.26.1932 [Código Eleitoral de 1932, Election Code of 1932].

3. Decreto no. 7.586, de 28 de Maio de 1945, DIÁRIO OFICIAL DA UNIÃO [D.O.U.] t.1: 9436 de 5.28.1945. (Lei Constitucional No. 9, 28/2/45 e Lei Constitucional No. 10, de 5 Dezembro de 1945).

4. *See* Hannah Maruci, *Women's Struggle to Vote in Brazil: Same Fight, Different Strategies*, OXFORD HUMAN RIGHTS HUB (Feb. 24, 2018), https://ohrh.law.ox.ac.uk/womens-struggle-to-vote-in-brazil-same-fight-different-strategies/.

5. SONIA ALVAREZ, ENGENDERING DEMOCRACY IN BRAZIL: WOMEN'S MOVEMENTS IN TRANSITION POLITICS 37, 51 (1990).

6. *Id.* at 51, 54.

while the government's economic policies gave rise to a wave of women's empowerment in Brazil.[7]

The Brazilian government's authoritarian approach pragmatically resulted in "the politicization of motherhood," with women becoming more aware of gender inequalities and socially constructed roles of women, as well as the consequences of those imposed roles on women's rights and empowerment.[8] Thus, political participation by women, while beginning in 1932, took root in the 1970s.[9]

The 1970s represented a milestone for women's rights in Brazil. Feminist ideology and the formation of women's groups expanded and gained strength.[10] Liberated feminists began to demand equal rights, access to careers, and societal changes to end domestic violence.

The reestablishment of a democratic government in the late 1980s helped efforts to close gender gaps and achieve positive gains for women.[11] The women's movement also catalyzed issues as part of the agendas of labor unions, community associations, and political parties.[12]

A transformative change arrived with the inclusion of gender equality principles in the 1988 Constitution and legal reforms to enforce the principles.[13] Among those, the new constitution guaranteed the right to family planning and access to childcare and preschool centers.[14] The constitution also included provisions to protect against family violence.[15]

With its 1988 Constitution, Brazil sought to harmonize domestic rights for women with its treaty-based obligations, such as the Convention on the Elimination of All Forms of Discrimination Against Women (CEDAW), which Brazil ratified in 1984.[16] Brazil later accepted the

---

7. *Id.* at 55.

8. *Id.* at 57.

9. *See* MARK O'DOHERTY, HEALING BRAZIL: A STUDY OF HUMAN RIGHTS VIOLATIONS, SOCIAL INEQUALITY, DEMOCRATIC DEFICIT AND DICTATORSHIP IN THE FEDERATIVE REPUBLIC OF BRAZIL 36 (2018).

10. *See* Rose-Marie Avin, *Engendering Development: A Critique*, *in* FEMINIST ECONOMICS AND THE WORLD BANK: HISTORY, THEORY AND POLICY 65, 70 (Edith Kuiper & Drucilla K. Barker eds., 1st ed. 2006).

11. *See id.*

12. *See id.*

13. *See* Renata Gukova et al., World Bank, A SNAPSHOT OF GENDER IN BRAZIL TODAY: INSTITUTIONS, OUTCOMES, AND A CLOSER LOOK AT RACIAL AND GEOGRAPHIC DIFFERENCES 5 (2006).

14. CONSTITUIÇÃO FEDERAL [C.F.] [Constitution] arts. 208, 226.

15. CONSTITUIÇÃO FEDERAL [C.F.] [Constitution] art. 226(8).

16. Convention on the Elimination of All Forms of Discrimination Against Women, Dec. 18, 1979, 1249 U.N.T.S. 13 (ratified by Brazil on Feb. 1, 1984).

Optional Protocol to CEDAW in 2002, recognizing the ability of the CEDAW Committee to monitor compliance with the treaty and to receive complaints from individuals or groups for violations of women's rights covered by the treaty.[17]

Close on its heels, the Brazilian Civil Code was updated in 2003 to ensure equal marital rights for men and women and equal age requirements, such as for retirement pension eligibility.[18]

To foster implementation of women's constitutional and legal rights to equality, Brazil created new institutions and gender-responsive programs, such as Women's Rights Councils, health programs for women, and mechanisms to address victims of sexual and domestic violence, including special women's police stations and domestic violence units within nonspecialized police stations.[19] Local, regional, and federal governments also sought contributions from civil society in the formulation of public policies related to women's issues.[20]

Bringing policy coherence, the national Secretariat for Women's Policies (SNPM) within the Ministry of Women, Family, and Human Rights is responsible for formulating, coordinating, and articulating public policies for women, including nondiscrimination and ending all forms of violence against women. The secretariat also designs and maintains national plans for women's policies.[21] Supporting the secretariat's work to promote gender equality and women's full participation in political, economic, and cultural activities is the National Council on Women's Rights (CNDM). The council's functions and structure have changed through the years since its creation in 1985 to include broader themes and expanded representation by various federal institutions and civil society.[22]

---

17. Optional Protocol to the Convention on the Elimination of All Forms of Discrimination Against Women, Oct. 6, 1999, 2131 U.N.T.S. 83 (acceptance by Brazil on June 28, 2002).

18. *See* Lei No. 10.406, de 10 de Janeiro de 2002, Diário Oficial da União [D.O.U.] de 11.1.2002 [Civil Code].

19. *See* Feminist Economics and the World Bank, *supra* note 10, at 70.

20. *See* Gukova et al., *supra* note 13, at 50.

21. *See Women's Policies*, Ministry of Women, Family & Human Rights, Braz. Gov't, https://www.gov.br/mdh/pt-br/navegue-por-temas/politicas-para-mulheres (last visited July 31, 2021).

22. *See* Decreto No. 10.174, de 13 Dezembro de 2019, Diário Oficial da União [D.O.U.] t.242: 69 de 16.12.2019 (amending structures and functions); Decreto No. 9.417, de 20 de Junho de 2018, Diário Oficial da União [D.O.U.] t.118: 1 de 21.6.2018 (transferring the Secretariat of Women's Policies to the Ministry of Women, Family, and Human Rights); Decreto No. 8.202, de 6 de Março de 2014, Diário Oficial da União [D.O.U.] t.1: 1 de 7.3.2014.

Despite the aforementioned achievements, how far is Brazil from gender equality nowadays?

The country still has a long way to go to ensure a real voice for Brazilian women. That voice is diverse. The women's rights agenda in Brazil includes a broad range of women—feminists, lesbians, Black women, domestic workers, unpaid workers, and women in poor living conditions, among others.[23] As such, when it comes to Brazil, there is a vast internal diversity that has to be taken into consideration, including racial and geographic differences.[24]

Today's tendency is to take women's right to vote for granted, yet important gender gaps remain.[25] Among those gaps, women in Brazil still face limited representation in politics. Brazil's elections law requires each political party to include a minimum of 30 percent women in their lists of candidates, but it does not impose a minimum of reserved seats for women.[26] As a result, the quota law does not guarantee a minimum percent or number of women elected. Practical experiences for more than two decades show that the aspirations of the quota policies have fallen short. Although it has been nearly 90 years since universal suffrage in Brazil, women occupy a paltry 15.2 percent of the lower chamber and 12.4 percent of the upper chamber in the National Congress, as of July 2021.[27]

As such, women remain marginalized from active participation in key legislative decisions affecting women's lives and the broader society in which they live.[28] For example, in 2017, a special congressional committee approved an amendment to the Brazilian Constitution to specify that life begins at conception, thereby effectively banning abortion under

23. *See* Gukova et al., *supra* note 13, at 5.

24. *See* Miriam Muller, *Getting Closer to Equal in Brazil? Yes, But . . .*, World Bank Blog (Mar. 10, 2017), https://blogs.worldbank.org/latinamerica/getting-closer-equal-brazil-yes.

25. *See* Sylvie Bossoutrot, Opinion, *Gender Equality: Why it Matters, Especially in a Time of Crisis*, World Bank, Apr. 13, 2020, https://www.worldbank.org/en/news/opinion/2020/04/13/gender-equality-why-it-matters-especially-in-a-time-of-crisis.

26. *See* Decreto No. 9.504, de 30 de Setembro de 1997, Diário Oficial da União [D.O.U.] t.1: 21801 de 10.1.1997.

27. *Monthly Ranking of Women in National Parliaments*, Inter-Parliamentary Union, https://data.ipu.org/women-ranking (last updated June 1, 2021).

28. *See* Mariana K. Ceratti, *What Does It Mean to Be a Woman in Brazil? The Answer Will Surprise You*, World Bank (Mar. 8, 2017), https://www.worldbank.org/en/news/feature/2017/03/08/ser-mujer-brasil.

all circumstances, including when the life of the woman is at risk.[29] The only woman on the committee voted against the amendment.[30]

Women are similarly underrepresented in the senior career diplomatic ranks within the Ministry of Foreign Affairs with only 17 women ambassadors compared to 200 men.[31]

In the workplace, women continue to face pay gaps for an equivalent job. Further, they are more likely to be employed in areas of lower economic growth and lower pay. Roughly 45 percent of employed women work in the food service, education, social services, and domestic services sectors, whereas 48 percent of employed men work in agriculture, manufacturing, and construction.[32]

As social scientist Miriam Muller asserts:

> But, it will not be possible to achieve equality in Brazil if we do not take it on in a nuanced way: Tackling racial and geographic inequalities is critical for the design of policies and projects. If we do not target and tailor the efforts, these will not be effective, and Afro-Brazilian women and those living in the northern parts of the country may be systematically left behind: They may continue to have less access to education and health services, to die at higher rates from pregnancy related issues, to have fewer and worse jobs, and to be more exposed to (deadly) violence than their white peers in the South and Southeast regions.[33]

Progress will require collecting data on the intersectional issues of gender, race, ethnicity, geography, and economic conditions and using that information to inform priorities for changes in policies, institutions, and legislation.[34] These changes must be met with effective implementation to expand gender equality, women's access to economic opportunities, and women's inclusion in political and social life. This includes and applies to laws and awareness raising so that we reach a broader scale and move closer to realizing gender equality and making it a lasting reality.[35]

---

29. *See* Ana Balbachevsky Guilhon Albuquerque, *Brazil's Gender Trouble: Sources of Inequality in Brazilian Institutions and Political Representation*, Ctr. for Feminist Foreign Policy J. (Dec. 8, 2017).

30. *See id.*

31. *See id.*

32. Ceratti, *supra* note 28.

33. Muller, *supra* note 24.

34. *See* Gukova et al., *supra* note 13, at 32.

35. *See* Paula Tavares, *How Does Brazilian Law See Women?*, World Bank Blog (Mar. 20, 2017), https://blogs.worldbank.org/latinamerica/how-does-brazilian-law-see-women.

4

Guatemala: Securing Equality and Full Political Participation by Women and Indigenous People

María Isabel Luján Zilbermann and Fernanda Monzón Arroyo[1]

Guatemala is a country with a rich cultural diversity framed in the 108,889 square kilometers of its extension, and whose Indigenous population represents 43.6 percent of the total population.[2] Although the urban population has grown since the last decades of the last century, the majority of people live in rural or semi-rural areas. All these elements have had a very important influence on the political participation of Guatemalan women, beginning with their right to vote.

The Guatemalan population is made up of a wide variety of peoples, among them the Maya, Garifuna, Xinka, and Ladino, many of whom have their own authorities and election mechanisms different from the universal suffrage contemplated in the Political Constitution of the Republic. In this chapter, we will focus on the vote of women and their political participation within the context of the constitutional legal order of Guatemala, as this is the life experience of the authors.

Guatemala's political past has been characterized by the intermittent influence of the Catholic Church on government issues and the dichotomy between liberal and conservative reformers. As a result of the Liberal Reform of 1871 and its religious laws, the Catholic Church was weakened

1. María Isabel Luján Zilbermann is a partner and Fernanda Monzón Arroyo is an associate at ALTA QIL+4 Abogados, a law firm in Guatemala.

2. *Resultados del Censo 2018 [Results from the Census 2018]*, NAT'L STATISTICS INST. OF GUAT., https://www.censopoblacion.gt/cuantossomos (last visited June 21, 2021) (Spanish).

both politically and economically. However, in 1944, more than 90 percent of the Guatemalan population declared themselves to be Catholic.[3]

From 1898 to 1944, the country was governed, for the most part, in a dictatorial and arbitrary way.[4] A lack of democratic experience sparked nationalist sentiments, and extremist and radical ideologies. After the October Revolution of 1944, a strong longing for democracy and social justice, as well as the search for the recognition of civic and political liberties and human rights, reigned in the country. This sentiment led to the creation of a new constitutional order whose pillars were fundamental principles of the 1944 Revolution, such as executive decentralization, non-reelection, the democratic organization of municipalities through popular elections, compulsory and secret suffrage for literate men, and the recognition of the citizenship of the "prepared woman."[5]

Women's Right to Vote

When the National Constituent Assembly of 1945 discussed suffrage and civic and political rights, there were those who remained reluctant to accept the idea of granting women the right to vote. In these conversations, proposals for restrictive amendments emerged, consisting of limiting the participation of women in municipal elections or even temporarily suspending the recognition of their right to vote. Opponents argued that women were "an easy instrument of religious sentimentality."[6]

However, the constituents decided not to punish women for fear of the influence of the Catholic Church. Although there were those who opposed it, the vast majority of the constituents were determined to grant the right to vote to Guatemalan women. Furthermore, according to the

3. *See* Hubert J. Miller, *La Iglesia Católica y el Protestantismo*, *in* 5 Historia General de Guatemala 261 (Jorge Luján Muñoz ed., Asociación de Amigos del País, Fundación para la Cultura y el Desarrollo 2d ed. 1999).

4. *See* J. Daniel Contreras R., *Introducción*, *in* 5 Historia General de Guatemala 3 (Jorge Luján Muñoz ed., Asociación de Amigos del País, Fundación para la Cultura y el Desarrollo 2d ed. 1999).

5. Jorge Mario García Laguardia, Constituciones Iberoamericanas: Guatemala 38 (Universidad Nacional Autónoma de México 2006), https://biblio.juridicas.unam.mx/bjv/detalle-libro/2210-constituciones-iberoamericanas-guatemala; *cf.* 333 Decreto del Congreso de la República, Boletín del Congreso, núm. 7, Guatemala, Tipografía Nacional, December 3, 1944 through February 1947.

6. Ana Patricia Borrayo Morales, Mujeres y Ciudadanía: Un Enfoque Histórico-Social Los Inicios 1921 y 1944, 46 (Apr. 2015) (unpublished thesis, Univ. de San Carlos de Guatemala).

1945 Constitutional Assembly Sessions Diary, the fear that totalitarian regimes left regarding the docility of the illiterate vote prompted the constituents to choose to limit the right to vote based on literacy. Thus, in 1945, the new constitution recognized women of legal age who knew how to read and write with the status of citizens with optional and secret voting rights.

Twenty years later, when the 1965 Constitution was drafted, the status of citizen was extended to all Guatemalan women over the age of 18. Consequently, the right to vote was granted to both literate women and those who could not read or write. In the case of literate women, the right to vote was compulsory, while for the illiterate, it was optional. It was not until the promulgation in 1985 of the current constitution that the election was conceived as a political duty, making the vote of all women mandatory and secret.

Despite the fact that women's voting and other political rights had been constitutionally guaranteed since 1985, Guatemalan women's political participation remained largely negligible through the end of the 20th century, with women comprising less than 10 percent of members of Congress in 2002.[7] Although there are those who attribute women's lagging political participation to the strong presence of conservative politicians in the government and in Congress, in reality, there has been little public data to corroborate the reason for the low participation of Guatemalan women in national elections. Further, understanding long-standing structural barriers to their participation has been difficult because, as a result of the coup d'état of March 1982, most of the public documents and records related to the elections and political parties were destroyed or disappeared.[8]

Throughout its history, Guatemalan society has been characterized by having a patriarchal family culture and organization. Despite the fact that this sentiment has progressively weakened in the last century, it remains in force today, particularly in the country's provinces. With certain exceptions, such as obtaining the presidency of the Congress of

---

7. Nineth Montenegro, *The Challenge of Women's Political Participation in Guatemala*, *in* Women in Parliament (International IDEA 2002) (English translation), https://www.idea.int/sites/default/files/publications/chapters/women-in-parliament/mujeres-en-el-parlamento-mas-alla-de-los-numeros-2002-EN-case-study-guatemala.pdf.

8. Arnoldo Daetz Call, *Elecciones y Partidos Políticos [Election and Political Parties]*, in 6 Historia General de Guatemala 87 (Jorge Luján Muñoz ed., Asociación de Amigos del País, Fundación para la Cultura y el Desarrollo 2d ed. 1999) (Spanish).

the Republic in 1991 and the first participation of a woman as part of the magistracy of the Supreme Electoral Tribunal (Tribunal Supremo Electoral, TSE) in 2008, as previously mentioned, the participation of women in the political life of Guatemala during the 1990s and the first decade of the 21st century was precarious.

Securing Women's Full Political Participation

Regardless of whether women's limited political participation in the past was due to the high levels of illiteracy in the country's female population, to the patriarchal organization of Guatemalan society, or to the conservatism that still occupies an important place in the country's institutions, to say that participation in Guatemala's political life is a male privilege would be a wrong statement that departs from the current reality. Although slowly and not without obstacles and resistance, since 2010, female participation in the country's elections has been constantly growing. This change can be attributed, among others, to two factors: (1) the issuance of the Personal Identification Document (DPI) and the creation of the National Registry of Persons, and (2) the increased transhumance of voters in the country.

Personal Identification Document

In 2004, Decree 10-04 introduced reforms to the Electoral and Political Parties Law that directly link the right to vote to the DPI.[9] Thus, the duty of all Guatemalan citizens to register in the Citizen Registry and to obtain the DPI was established, which empowers each citizen to exercise the right to vote. Article 7 of the law also provided that citizenship may be proven exclusively with the DPI, and no longer with the document known as Cédula de Vecindad, which was issued by the applicable Civil Registry of the more than 300 municipalities that exist in Guatemala.

National Registry of Persons

The following year, the Congress of the Republic issued Decree 90-2005, which contains the Law on the National Registry of Persons (RENAP).[10]

---

9. 10-2004 Decreto del Congreso de la República, Diario de Centro América Guatemala, núm. 29, Guatemala, Tipografía Nacional, May 25, 2004 (reforming the Electoral and Political Parties Law, Decree 1-85).

10. 90-2005 Decreto del Congreso de la República, Diario de Centro América Guatemala, núm. 28, Guatemala, Tipografía Nacional, December 21, 2005 (reforming the Electoral and Political Parties Law, Decree 1-85).

One of the main objectives of this law was to implement technology that would automate the information related to natural persons, such as name, sex, location, date of birth, and marital status, so that registration procedures would be unified throughout the country. In addition, the regulation sought to regulate the issuance of the DPI. This law established the obligation of coordination between the TSE and RENAP, and affirmed the DPI as the only valid identification document for a Guatemalan citizen to use when exercising the right to vote.

Starting in August 2010, RENAP began issuing DPIs to Guatemalan citizens. Registry automation and technological updating in the registration procedure had immediate forceful effects. For the last elections that were carried out with the archaic system of the Cédula de Vecindad in 2007, the electoral records registered by the TSE totaled 5,990,031 Guatemalans.[11] In 2011, one year after the first DPIs were issued in the country, the electoral roll totaled 7,340,841, an increase of 22.5 percent compared to the 2007 elections.[12] Furthermore, the percentage of women registered in the country also increased significantly. While in 2007, women represented 47 percent of the electoral roll, in 2011, women represented 51 percent of Guatemalans registered in the country.[13]

Electoral Transhumance

Another element of the Guatemalan reality that has influenced the increasing participation of women in national suffrage is the electoral transhumance. Electoral transhumance consists of the transfer of voters from the place where they reside to another, and the registration of false data, such as the place of residence, to alter the electoral roll and thereby benefit a candidate for a certain municipal or departmental office.

This practice was used with such frequency in the general elections in Guatemala that the TSE received complaints of electoral transhumance before the general elections of 2007, 2011, and 2015. As a consequence, in 2016, Article 13 of the Electoral and Political Parties Law, which recognizes the absolute freedom of citizens to cast their votes, was modified, adding to it that "[t]he transfer of voters from one municipality to another,

11. *Election Guide: Republic of Guatemala, Election for Congress 2007*, IFES, https://www.electionguide.org/elections/id/1482/ (last visited June 21, 2021).

12. *Election Guide: Republic of Guatemala, Election for Congress 2011*, IFES, https://www.electionguide.org/elections/id/1602/ (last visited June 21, 2021).

13. *Statistics of the Electoral Register by Department and Municipalities*, Supreme Electoral Tribunal (TSE), https://www.tse.org.gt (search statistics to compare 2007 and 2011) (last visited June 21, 2021).

processing the change of their electoral residence in a fictitious manner is sanctioned in accordance with the law."[14]

Increasing Women's Participation in Parliament and Public Offices

In the country's last elections in 2019, women represented 54 percent of the electoral roll.[15] However, the Observation Report by the Electoral Observation Mission of the Organization of American States (OAS Mission) highlighted the unequal participation of women and Indigenous people in Guatemalan politics.[16] Despite the fact that the voices of women constitute the majority of voters, women currently represent only 19.4 percent of members of Guatemala's Congress for the period 2020–2024.[17] This figure is below the regional average of 32.4 percent[18] and reflects the challenges to political participation faced by women in Guatemala.

Likewise, the Observation Report indicated that the OAS Mission received complaints from female candidates who received threats and were victims of hate messages. This discrimination was accentuated in the case of women in public office, who were attacked both in person and through their social networks. In the case of Indigenous women, the attacks adopted a racist tone in addition to the discriminatory tone. In view of the foregoing, the OAS Mission recommended enacting legislation on gender-based political violence.[19]

There are still several areas for improvement in the political representation of women in Guatemala, and there must be a full commitment from the state to implement the necessary measures. However, action to achieve progress for women's rights is not reserved to those in government. Guatemala is a country with a predominantly young

---

14. 26-2016 Decreto del Congreso de la República, Diario de Centro América Guatemala, núm. 69, Guatemala, Tipografía Nacional, May 25, 2016 (reforming the Electoral and Political Parties Law, Decree 1-85).

15. *Statistics of the Electoral Register by Department and Municipalities*, SUPREME ELECTORAL TRIBUNAL (TSE), https://www.tse.org.gt/ (search statistics for 2019) (last visited June 21, 2021).

16. OAS, FINAL REPORT OF THE ELECTORAL OBSERVATION MISSION FOR REPUBLIC OF GUATEMALA ELECTIONS 2019, at 25–29 (Nov. 18, 2020), http://scm.oas.org/pdfs/2020/CP43280EFINALREPORTMOAS.pdf.

17. *Id.* at 25; *Monthly Ranking of Women in National Parliaments*, INTER-PARLIAMENTARY UNION, https://data.ipu.org/women-ranking (last updated June 1, 2021).

18. *Global and Regional Averages of Women in National Parliaments*, INTER-PARLIAMENTARY UNION, https://data.ipu.org/women-averages (last updated June 1, 2021).

19. OAS, *supra* note 16, at 27.

population—54.7 percent are under the age of 24, of which 51.5 percent are female. The new generations that have been born under a constitutional regime without distinction between genders have a very clear perspective on the importance of balanced and equal participation between men and women. We consider that, with the appropriate approach and the strengthening of democratic institutions, women's active political participation in Guatemala will bring unmatched and positive value in the years to come.

5

India: The Electoral Landscape and the Glass Ceiling in the World's Largest Democracy

Arya Tripathy and Priti Suri[1]

India is the world's largest democracy and yet is categorized as a "flawed democracy," ranking 53 out of 167 countries and territories in the Economist Intelligence Unit Democracy Index 2020.[2] The erosion of India's democratic mosaic is gradual and can be largely attributed to a systematic disregard of minority political and civil rights. This unpromising scenario is despite the Indian electorate size being equivalent to the combined electorates of 36 democracies with an average annual increase of 11.2 percent since 1952.[3] While the majority of the credited debates around Indian democracy focus on deprivation of religious minorities' civil and political rights, the approach may be viewed as an oversimplification of the diverse polity and its multitude of issues. Indian political bifurcation and resultant discrimination are premised on a variety of factors, such as caste, class, language, and gender. The state has enacted several laws that strive to bring societal, cultural, and economic parity between the two sexes, but there is a vacuum in undertaking affirmative actions to ensure

1. Arya Tripathy is partner at PSA, a law firm in India. Priti Suri is the founder and managing partner of PSA and recipient of the 2017 American Bar Association International Law Section's Mayre Rasmussen Award for the Advancement of Women in International Law.

2. *Democracy Index 2020*, The Economist Group, https://www.eiu.com/topic/democracy-index (last visited June 21, 2021).

3. Srinivasan Ramani & Vignesh Radhakrishnan, *World Within a Country: The Size of India's Electorate in Four Charts*, The Hindu (Mar. 12, 2019, 15:57 IST; updated May 2, 2019, 15:42 IST), https://www.thehindu.com/data/indias-electorate-as-big-as-36-countries/article26507627.ece.

equality in women's participation in the electoral process. Undeniably, true representation in Indian democracy requires women's participation not just in the suffrage process. It also calls for their increased participation in actual decision-making and pre-poll processes in order to bring sustainable overall development that reflects women citizens' aspirations.

In this chapter, we provide an overview of India's electoral structure and process and analyze the degree of women's political participation from a right-to-vote and a right-to-contest matrix. For our analysis, we have relied on secondary information sources available publicly, including government data, private survey findings, academic research, and scholarly articles.

Overview of Electoral Structure and Process

India is a federal republic that follows a three-layered government structure: central, state, and local. Each state has multiple constituencies, and the electoral process for the first two tiers is based on these constituencies. For local governments, the process is conducted at the village and city levels. At the national level, elections for the Parliament's lower house, *Lok Sabha*, are through general elections held every five years by universal adult suffrage. India has seen 17 Lok Sabha elections, with the last one held in 2019. Members of Parliament's upper house, *Rajya Sabha*, are elected by an electoral college comprised of members of Lok Sabha, and state and union territory legislative assemblies. At the state level, similar structures and election processes are in place for both houses of each state's legislative assemblies (called *Vidhan Sabha* and *Vidhan Parishad*). The third tier of local governance at the village (*Panchayats*) and municipal corporation (*Nagarpalika*) levels also follows an electoral process every five years.

The elections for the three tiers are regulated and supervised by Election Commissions (ECs), which are permanent and independent statutory bodies constituted at the national and state levels. Each EC is responsible for conducting elections, collecting data on registered voters, preparing electoral rolls, calculating polls, providing electoral infrastructure such as booths and electronic voting machines, registration of political parties, nomination of electoral candidates, and monitoring election campaigns and political funding. Prior to polls at an election, each EC publishes data on political parties, candidates, and voters per constituency. At the end of every national and state-level election, each EC collates and publishes data on votes cast, forfeited, and nullified and on poll results.

Women's Right to Vote

Article 326 of the Indian Constitution states that elections to the parliament and state legislative assemblies shall be on the basis of universal "adult suffrage." Every Indian citizen who is 18 years old or older is entitled to vote in the electoral process, unless disqualified under law on grounds of nonresidence, unsoundness of mind, crime, and illegal or corrupt practices. Universal adult suffrage is not a fundamental right,[4] but its contours are fortified by Articles 14 and 15 of the Indian Constitution, which vest every citizen with the fundamental right to equality and equal protection of law. A qualified adult can vote freely and fairly, without discrimination on the basis of religion, race, caste, sex, place of birth, class, and ethnicity. Any law that seeks to limit or restrict the suffrage right of an individual based on sex criteria will attract strict constitutional scrutiny as being violative of the right to equality.

Further, in order to ensure free and fair elections as a fundamental facet of Indian democracy, Part XV of the Indian Constitution (Articles 324–329) allows the central and state governments to make laws for all matters connected with elections. Pursuant to this, the Representation of the People Acts of 1950 and 1951 (RPA) were enacted.[5] The RPA provides for the allocation of seats in central and state legislatures, delimitation of constituencies, preparation of electoral rolls, and qualification of voters. As per this, a citizen is a voter in his/her resident constituency, except those who are judicially declared as of unsound mind or are convicted for certain crimes and corruption. Apart from the RPA, the state governments are required to make laws on local government elections, and each state has enacted its own Panchayati Raj/municipalities acts. Consequently, Indian women have been vested with the right to vote freely since 1950, much before many other democracies.

Women's Right to Contest

Unlike the right to vote, the right to contest elections is not a constitutional right. It is a legal right under the RPA and applicable local government laws. Any citizen desirous of contesting an election must fulfill the criteria laid out therein. An eligible citizen can contest either as affiliated

4. *See, e.g.*, K. Krishna Murthy & Ors. v. Union of India (2010) 7 S.C.C. 202.

5. *See* Representation of the People Act, 1950, No. 43, Acts of Parliament, 1950; Representation of the People Act, 1951, No. 43, Acts of Parliament, 1951.

to a political party or as an independent candidate. Prior to contesting, a citizen must be a registered elector and disclose details regarding antecedents, assets, educational qualifications, and other details. The RPA and local government laws list out various grounds for disqualification, and each EC verifies the eligibility before approving election candidature.

Nonetheless, the eligibility criteria under these laws are subject to judicial review, and there are a plethora of cases where candidature conditions are scrutinized on constitutional principles of reasonableness and equality. For instance, in *Rajabala v. State of Haryana*, the provisions of the Haryana Panchayati Raj (Amendment) Act, 2015, that disqualified candidates without specified educational qualifications was challenged as being violative of the right to equality under Article 14 of the Indian Constitution.[6] The petitioner contended that 50 percent of Haryana's rural population, especially women, would be disqualified due to the generally low levels of education in the state. As a result, such disqualification criteria would be prejudicial to women candidates. It was contended that the criteria did not have any legitimate purpose, except for creating an unrealistic bifurcation at the grassroots level. The Indian Supreme Court acknowledged the low levels of education but upheld the constitutional validity of the criteria. The Supreme Court reasoned that the candidature's educational qualification had a bearing on his ability to discharge public functions as part of the local government, was essential for better decision-making, and, hence, was not violative of the right to equality. To sum up, women can contest elections in India for different tiers as long as they meet the eligibility criteria under law.

Women's Political Participation

Based on the preceding framework analysis, Indian women have equal suffrage rights and the right to contest elections. The questions that arise here are: Is it that simple, and can Indian polity be viewed as gender inclusive? The answers will require a deeper dive into the overall degree of women's political participation in India. This evaluation must have a wider ambit, and we believe it should account for (1) women's voter turnout; (2) candidacy rates and participation in elections; (3) involvement in election campaigning and electoral behavior as deciphered from the extent of awareness, interest in politics, and freedom to exercise electoral choices, among other factors; and (4) gender-stereotyped roles for elected women candidates. The subsequent sections analyze each of these aspects.

6. *See* Rajabala v. State of Haryana (2016) 2 S.C.C. 445.

Women's Voter Turnout

The origins of women's suffrage in India can be traced to the pre-independence era, where the equal franchise right was introduced by the British.[7] The post-independence narrative was influenced by India's independence movement, nationalist ideals, and politico-legal requirements for India. Since 1952, and over the course of 17 elections to Lok Sabha, Indian polity has witnessed a sea change in the electoral suffrage base and the number of votes cast by women. Until the third Lok Sabha elections of 1962, there was hardly any authentic statistical source that could be relied on to compare the existing scenario. The third Lok Sabha elections witnessed a total 55.4 percent voter turnout (out of about 216 million registered voters) for 494 constituencies, of which women's voter turnout stood at 46.6 percent.[8] Fast forward to the 17th Lok Sabha elections of 2019: 67.0 percent (out of about 910 million registered voters) was the total turnout for 542 constituencies, of which women's voter turnout stood at 67.2 percent.[9] The surge in numbers indicates that the number of women voters in India has exponentially risen over the last 48 years, and the political parties acknowledge the need for canvassing their votes to win requisite political majority.

In the backdrop of these promising numbers, it must be highlighted that the trend is not influenced by a top-down law or policy approach. India does not have any compulsory voting obligation for its citizens, nor does it have dedicated policies to incentivize women voters to participate in polls. In the absence of such legal measures, the statistics create an impression that India has witnessed systematic reduction of gender bias in voting, where women voters feel self-empowered. It may also indicate that women are increasingly aware of the significance of their electoral participation and that the government has created a conducive voting environment that facilitates their freedom to vote.[10] However, analysis of women's empowerment in politics will be half-hearted without accounting for the entire political scenario.

7. Praveen Rai, *Electoral Participation of Women in India: Key Determinants and Barriers*, 46 Econ. & Poli. Wkly. 47, 49 (Jan. 15, 2011), https://www.csds.in/uploads/custom_files/1529066526_Electoral%20Participation%20of%20Women%20in%20India.pdf.

8. Election Comm'n of India, 1 Report on the Third General Elections in India 1962 47, 74 (1965), https://indianculture.gov.in/flipbook/2536.

9. *Highlights for Elections 2019: 17 LOK SABHA*, Election Comm'n of India (Oct. 11, 2019), https://eci.gov.in/files/file/10991-2-highlights/.

10. *See generally* Mudit Kapoor & Shamika Ravi, *Women Voters in Indian Democracy: A Silent Revolution*, 49 Econ. & Poli. Wkly. 63 (Mar. 22, 2014), https://www.indiaspend.com/wp-content/uploads/2019/03/Kapoor-Ravi-2014.pdf.

Women's Election Candidature

While women are an essential vote bank for political parties, the same cannot be confirmed when it comes to inducting women into party ranks and electoral candidature base. According to the Inter-Parliamentary Union 2020 ranking, India is 149th out of 193 countries in terms of women's representation in its lower house of parliament, having only 14.4 percent women in the Lok Sabha.[11] In comparison, women's representation in other neighboring South Asian countries like Afghanistan (27.0 percent), Bangladesh (20.9 percent), Nepal (32.7 percent), and Pakistan (20.2 percent) is at or beyond 20 percent, a critical-mass threshold for gender parity in political decision-making.[12] The skewed participation of women as election candidates is also evidenced from Lok Sabha elections per-poll data collated by the national EC. Table 1 provides year-wise data for the total number of seats contested, as contrasted with the number of women candidates contesting for those seats over the last five general elections. Table 2 provides women's candidature from a few select national parties as seen over the last two decades.

Table 1: Women's Candidature in Lok Sabha Elections

Lok Sabha election	Total number of seats	Number of women members	Percent of the total
Thirteenth (1999)	543	48	8.8
Fourteenth (2004)	543	45	8.1
Fifteenth (2009)	543	59	10.9
Sixteenth (2014)	543	62	11.41
Seventeenth (2019)	542	78	14.3

Source: Election Commission of India, Election Law Reports 1999–2019[13]

11. *Monthly Ranking of Women in National Parliaments*, INTER-PARLIAMENTARY UNION, https://data.ipu.org/women-ranking (last updated Apr. 1, 2021).

12. *Id.*; *cf.* Rai, *supra* note 7, at 47, 50, 54 (discussing how the world average of 20 percent is the "critical mass" required to introduce gender parity in political decision-making), https://www.csds.in/uploads/custom_files/1529066526_Electoral%20Participation%20of%20Women%20in%20India.pdf.

13. *Election Law Reports 1999-2019*, ELECTION COMM'N OF INDIA, https://www.elections.in/parliamentary-constituencies/1962-election-results.html (search by year) (last visited June 21, 2021).

Table 2: Women's Candidature from Select National Parties

Party	1999	2009	2019
Bhartiya Janata Party	25	44	55
Indian National Congress	51	45	54
Communist Party of India	4	4	4
Communist Party of India (Marxist)	5	6	10

Source: Election Commission of India, Election Law Reports 1999–2019[14]

The numbers unravel an abysmally low rate of increase over time, thereby keeping women majorly excluded from the actual decision-making and politico-legal process. Political parties cite women candidates' lack of "winnability" as a key reason for their limited participation.[15] However, statistics again discredit this assertion. In the 15th Lok Sabha elections of 2009, the success rate for women candidates was 10.6 percent (59 of 556), while that of men was 6.4 percent (484 of 7,514).[16] In the 2019 elections, women scored 10.8 percent (78 out of 724) and men scored 6.4 percent (464 of 7,296).[17] These numbers substantiate that women have consistently maintained a higher "winnability" rate than their men counterparts. Thus, there have to be other social, economic, and cultural reasons for the evident female marginalization in party politics. In our opinion, there are three key reasons.

First, national political and regional parties have a deep-rooted "patriarchal mindset," which manifests in discrimination against women nominees as party representatives. This gender bias also marks internal party ranks and chain of command. The discrimination is strengthened by gender stereotyping, where women are regarded as incapable of holding public offices and decision-making positions. Hence, it is not a surprise that political parties still hold on to biases while deciding their respective representation and positions of power. However, recent judicial decisions recognizing women's economic rights are having an impact on changing that mindset. For instance, Indian armed forces did not allow permanent

14. *Id.*

15. Ctr. for the Study of Developing Societies, Women & Politics: Changing Trends and Emerging Patterns (2019), https://www.lokniti.org/otherstudies/women-politics-changing-trends-and-emerging-patterns-209.

16. Rajeshwari Deshpande, *How Did Women Vote in Lok Sabha Elections 2009*, 44 Econ. & Pol. Wkly. 83 (2009).

17. *Record 78 Women MPs in New Lok Sabha*, The Econ. Times (May 24, 2019, 6:18 PM IST), https://economictimes.indiatimes.com/news/elections/lok-sabha/india/record-78-women-mps-in-new-lok-sabha/articleshow/69484777.cms.

commissioning for women until February 2020, and the Indian Supreme Court in the landmark case of *Secretary, Ministry of Defence v. Babita Puniya & Ors*[18] observed that such discrimination was violative of the right to equality under Article 14 of the Indian Constitution. The government argued that "troops are not yet mentally schooled to accept women officers in command of units" basing the distinction on gender stereotypes, and the Supreme Court, rejecting such arguments, held that women are eligible to hold positions as commanding officers and for permanent commissions. The case has been celebrated as a step toward overcoming outdated and entrenched gender stereotypes that have discriminated against Indian women and as making a significant crack in the glass ceiling.

Second, party membership and nomination decisions in India are not only gender-biased but also colored by considerations of caste, religion, and class, which are engrained in India's vote bank politics.[19] That is, political parties prefer wooing votes based on caste, class, and religion, and prioritize these communities' representations over women. This approach moves beyond subconscious bias and is a deliberate attempt to discriminate against women.

Third, unlike many countries that mandate quotas for women's representation at federal and state levels, India does not have any such law. The Indian "political reservation" debate at the state and national levels continues to remain unresolved. The government proposed the Constitution (108th Amendment) Bill, commonly referred to as the Women's Reservation Bill, in 2008 to reserve 33 percent of all seats in the Lok Sabha and state legislative assemblies for women.[20] The bill was passed by the Rajya Sabha in 2010 but faced stern opposition in the Lok Sabha. As of June 2021, the bill had not yet been passed. However, the bill has encouraged action by political parties. For example, the head of the Biju Janata Dal national party announced a 33 percent reservation for women in 2019 and, in December 2020, reaffirmed the demand for passage of the Women's Reservation Bill.[21] Also, two regional parties achieved more

---

18. (2020) 7 S.C.C. 469.

19. *See, e.g.*, Abhijit Banerjee et al., *Growing Cleavages in India? Evidence from the Changing Structure of Electorates* (WID.world Working Paper No. 2019/05), https://wid.world/document/growing-cleavages-in-india-evidence-from-the-changing-structure-of-party-electorates-1962-2014-wid-world-working-paper-2019-05/.

20. Women's Reservation Bill [The Constitution (108th Amendment) Bill, 2008] (passed by Rajya Sabha Mar. 9, 2010), https://prsindia.org/billtrack/womens-reservation-bill-the-constitution-108th-amendment-bill-2008-45.

21. *See BJD Will Make Women Reservation a Major National Issue: Naveen Patnaik*, NDTV (Dec. 26, 2020, 4:40 pm IST), https://www.ndtv.com/india-news

than 33 percent representation by women in 2019. The Trinamool Congress in West Bengal fielded 14 of 42 candidates (40.5 percent), and the Biju Janta Dal in Odisha gave tickets to seven women out of 19 candidates (36.8 percent).[22]

The system of reserving seats for women is not unprecedented in India. The 73rd and 74th Constitutional Amendments of 1992 introduced Articles 243D and 243T to the Indian Constitution, mandating reservation of "not less than one-third" of the total number of seats for women at the local government level.[23] These have facilitated an increase in women's representation at the grassroots level. As per the Ministry of Statistics and Planning's report published in 2020, women's representation at the local government level (districts, intermediate blocks, and villages) stands at 44.4 percent.[24] This is higher than the mandated one-third seats and a better participation rate than the paltry 14.3 percent at the national level in the Lok Sabha elections in 2019.

Additionally, it is important to highlight here that the Indian judiciary has zealously guarded the constitutional protections for ensuring that women's representation at local government levels is not compromised due to socio-economic considerations. For instance, courts have ordered maintaining an office vacancy at the village panchayat level until such time as a suitable woman candidate is identified,[25] ruled against proxy representation in meetings by a relative of a woman representative,[26] and struck down disqualifications imposed on a woman representative owing to conduct of any other family member.[27] In light of this, it can be argued that women's reservations can yield better participation by women and allow courts to exercise judicial review over practices that seek to exclude them. Needless to say, adoption of reservation mandates, such as those proposed in the Women's Reservation Bill, will obligate political parties

/bjd-will-make-women-reservation-a-major-national-issue-odisha-cm-naveen-patnaik-2343940.

22. *How Many Women Candidates Will Contest in 2019?*, The Wire (Apr. 5, 2019), https://thewire.in/women/women-candidates-parliament.

23. India Const. art. 243D, §§ 2–4; 243T §§ 2–3.

24. Ministry of Statistics & Programme Implementation, Report on Women and Men in India 2019 107 (Mar. 31, 2020).

25. *See* Suresh Balkrishna Pogale v. State of Maharashtra (2004) (1) Bom.C.R. 821.

26. *See* Souninder Singh Hooda v. State of Uttaranchal & Ors., 2006 (deciding Writ Petition No. 353 of 2004 (M/B), High Court of Uttarakhand).

27. *See* Sau. Pramila v. Bandu, 2014 (6) Bom.C.R. 441.

at higher government levels to provide women with adequate representation and, over time, dilute the exclusionary trend.

Women's Participation in the Political Process

Apart from electoral representation, it is important to assess the extent of women's participation in election campaigns, pre-polling processes, and their general attitude toward politics. This kind of participation requires closer and multilevel interaction, greater mobility, time investments, financial and nonfinancial resources, and active support from friends and family. There is no official survey or statistics that account for these trends in India, which, quite naturally, raises some speculation on whether women actually have a voice in political processes. According to a study conducted by the Centre for the Study of Developing Societies (CSDS), an autonomous social science research institute based out of Delhi, in collaboration with Konrad Adenauer Stiftung, women's participation in election-related activities is limited.[28] The report surveys a sample of 6,348 women across 11 states and provides insights into pre-polling matters, awareness, interest in politics, preferred political party, politics as a career option, and other similar data points. The report highlights that 61 percent of the respondents would shy away from a career in politics and 50 percent believe that women from upper castes and wealthier and political backgrounds have an advantage. The report also points out that various socio-economic and cultural factors such as patriarchal societal and family structures; household responsibilities; cultural beliefs; financial constraints; lack of interest in politics; and absence of access to information around electoral systems, party politics, and processes hinder their participation.

Based on these findings, women's active political participation cannot be achieved unless historic notions around women's roles in society, culture, and the economy are addressed. The Indian government constantly aims at devising policies and laws that will enable equal opportunities and protections for women from oppressive practices. However, suffice it to say that implementation of these initiatives has constantly faced challenges, and it will be some time in India before women and men are clothed as equals.

Elected Women and Gender Stereotypes

There is consensus that the lack of representation of women in key and critical decision-making positions results in the sidelining of a women's

28. *See generally* CTR. FOR THE STUDY OF DEVELOPING SOCIETIES, *supra* note 15.

agenda and sustainable development goals.[29] For instance, a UNICEF background paper suggests that women are more inclined to adopt liberal policies as compared to men.[30] Women leaders in India are likely to focus more on social, health, and environmental goals, such as increased spending for education, health care, nutrition, and other areas benefiting women and children, such as drinking water.[31] Based on the central government's portfolio allocations over the past few years, elected women representatives are charged with perceived "feminine" ministries, such as culture, children and women's affairs, education, and minority affairs, while their men counterparts are entrusted with critical ministries, such as finance, defense, law, information technology, and infrastructure. Thus, it does not come as a surprise that India, in its 72 years of independence as a democracy, has had only one woman as president, as prime minister, and as ministers of defense, external affairs, and railways. The current finance minister is the second woman, but the first to hold the post full time. Overall, when women get elected, there generally has been a stereotyping of what portfolios they deserve and what goals they should advocate for. As a result, critical policies and laws that have a larger bearing on women's social and economic well-being have been largely shaped by men's viewpoints, with women politicians blocked from influential positions by the glass ceiling.

The Women's Reservation Debate

As discussed earlier, India's reservation policy for women in the political machinery is limited to local governments. The 1992 constitutional amendments, which were adopted with a view to enabling women's participation from scheduled castes and tribes, require that, of the one-third reserved seats for women, one-third should be reserved for women from these special communities.[32] Each term of office is five years,[33] and elections are conducted by the state EC. States have been empowered to promulgate their own legislation elaborating on the reservation percentage, disqualification criteria, electoral process, self-governance powers, maintenance of accounts, audits, and other functions for local governments. Despite their affirmative inclusion, there are practical problems,

29. *Cf.* Rai, *supra* note 7, at 47, 50, 54.

30. *See* Lori Beaman et al., *Background Paper on the State of Children: Women Politicians, Gender Bias and Policy-Making in Rural India* 1, 3 (UNICEF 2007).

31. *Id.*

32. India Const. art. 243D, §§ 2–4; 243T §§ 1–3.

33. *Id.* art. 83(2).

including proxy attendance by relatives of elected members, intimidation of and threats against elected women candidates' physical safety, and a lack of majority backing in the decision-making process. These problems are unique to rural and suburban areas and, thus, call for devising better implementation strategies. Nonetheless, the affirmative action of the 1992 constitutional amendments definitely has facilitated women's participation in economic development, social justice, and self-governance at local levels.

Unlike reservations at the local level, Indian polity has long been at the crossroads of providing reservations at the central and state levels. In 2021, 57 countries had legislated women's reservations in the lower or single house of their legislatures,[34] yet India's Women's Reservation Bill has been in limbo for more than a decade. Political parties have relegated it to the status of an election "agenda," and resonances are heard only when women's votes need to be capitalized upon for an advantage. The bill proposes adding a new Article 330A to the Indian Constitution to require the reservation of seats in the Lok Sabha and state assemblies on a rotational basis. Similar to the 1992 constitutional amendments, the bill would also mandate that the reserved women's representation include 33 percent reservation for women from scheduled castes and tribes. Each seat would be reserved only once in three consecutive general elections; the system of reservations would expire 15 years from the commencement date.

There are two main arguments against the Women's Reservation Bill. First, a reservation for women will disqualify eligible men who may be objectively better suited for seats. This reasoning has an inherent gender-biased assumption that men may be better qualified than women. It overlooks that a 33 percent reservation still allows a 67 percent level playing field for the men candidates. Second, some argue that, with the existing reservations for scheduled castes and tribes accounting for 131 out of 543 Lok Sabha seats, an additional 33 percent reservation will provide a disproportionate representation of people's wishes. This argument deserves some consideration, and it may be worthwhile to account for the women representatives from scheduled communities and to tally up community-specific quotas as well. As it may be, the question arises whether there is an alternative solution. The opponents suggest that political parties must adopt a "bottom-up" approach to induct more women candidates. In a way, they simply shun the idea of any law that obligates them to an inclusive

34. *See Gender Quotas Database: Legislated Candidate Quotas*, IDEA, https://www.idea.int/data-tools/data/gender-quotas/legislative-overview (last visited June 21, 2021).

political ecosystem. The historical evidence is abundant in showing that gender gaps are entrenched and walking the talk is extremely difficult for political parties. In our view, the passage of the Women's Representation Bill is long overdue for qualitative, diverse, and proportionate people's representation. Reservations for women cannot be the solution in the long run but will definitely provide an equitable basis for women to elevate out of their current plight.

The Way Forward

In order to tackle the delicate issues around women's participation in Indian politics, it is of paramount importance that every stakeholder in the political space—government, voters, candidates, political parties, the ECs, and courts—acknowledge that equal opportunity for women is far from reality in the world's biggest democracy. Acceptance of the existing gender divide will pave the way for awareness, voicing of opinions, and action. Some of the immediate steps that could facilitate this movement include:

- Pass the Women's Reservation Bill, taking into consideration the pros and cons of women's reservations at the national and state levels;
- Initiate government-funded campaigns to advance gender equality and gender-responsive policies within political parties;
- Expand training programs to help more women run for office, re-contest, and participate fully and effectively in all aspects of the political process;
- Conduct ongoing surveys on women-specific issues, particularly as related to women's political empowerment;
- Engage in open public consultation processes for policy initiatives and foster inclusive mechanisms to enable meaningful participation by women;
- Expand funding for and access to information and technology infrastructure, with a view to ensuring that everyone, regardless of class, social status, and geographical region, has access to political information and processes without physical barriers and mobility challenges;
- Enhance the use of digital governance to ensure that women representatives are better equipped to participate in decision-making processes despite socio-economic and geographical barriers;
- Increase the use of advanced analytics and big data to support policy making and our understanding of women's political participation and empowerment;

- Strengthen the pipeline for women's political engagement and leadership through increased education of women and girls about their legal rights, political processes, and the importance of women's involvement in public decision-making; and
- Focus on qualitative data collation and analysis to bring more insights on the role of women politicians, such as laws proposed by women parliamentarians, and parliament discussions on women's issues, among others.

Conclusion

India has made positive strides over the past years to increase suffrage awareness among women citizens. However, until women effectively amalgamate at all levels of the electoral process, India's development will continue to be a male narrative. India must overcome the persistent dearth of women politicians, candidates, and ministers and must end the entrenched visible stereotyping of women's roles and responsibilities in governance structures. Closing the political gender gap in India will require women's rights advocates to generate stronger momentum for ensuring the full and effective political participation of women, better political accountability to women, and a fully gender-inclusive electoral landscape. Further, as much as there is need for affirmative action by the government and within institutions, it is even more vital that political parties, society, and families embrace the importance and role of gender equality as a pillar of democracy. Now is the time for action to shape the future of India as an effective, accountable, and inclusive democracy, one in which all of its citizens, women and men, are empowered to participate in economic, social, and political life.

6

Iran: Culture, Political Participation, and Continuing Efforts

Shima Rostami[1]

History suggests that all around the world, in every era, governments, be they secular or religious, took advantage of the societal phenomenon of women's suffrage to fuel their political agendas. For example, at one time, women were challenged to consider women's suffrage as their right and later as a civic duty and responsibility. Iranian women's status, rights, and the right to vote have been complicated. To have a better understanding of the issue, this chapter provides a brief history of women's rights and voting status from an international perspective and then from two different eras in Iran—a part of the Qajar era and the Constitutional Revolution from the mid-19th century to 1925, and the Pahlavi era from 1925 to 1979. There are controversial debates concerning women's rights and status in current Iran, after the Islamic Revolution of 1979. For a variety of reasons, this chapter does not address the contemporary era, as it requires further in-depth discussions.

The Core of Women's Suffrage Movements: Women Are Fully Human

It is impossible to understand what it has meant to Iranian women to earn the right to vote and to face their challenges in exercising that right without considering the global perspective concerning the acculturation women experienced in different parts of the world. In fact, while the

1. Shima Rostami, EdD, is Executive Director of Gateway Human Trafficking and an adjunct faculty at the University of Missouri in St. Louis (UMSL) Sociology Department. The views expressed are the author's personal views.

suffering that women have gone through to amplify their voices might be different, in general, the cultures follow the same path: "Women are pushed into being nurturing, and men are pushed into and are perceived as being righteous."[2]

Nearly 100 years ago, Sigmund Freud claimed that women "show less sense of justice than men, that they [women] are less ready to submit to the great exigencies of life, that they are more often influenced in their judgments by feelings of affection or hostility."[3] However, in 1982, Carol Gilligan expanded on this to state that "women not only define themselves in a context of human relationship but also judge themselves in terms of their ability to care."[4]

In their different voices, women have been echoing one melody—that they have a right to play a role in shaping the world; that they are capable of making rational decisions; and that being compassionate and caring can coexist with being righteous and just!

In 1958, midway between Freud's and Gilligan's writings, Lawrence Kohlberg decided to develop his own ideas on Piaget's (1932) theory of moral development. After about 20 years of case studying, in the late 1970s, in developing his theory of moral development, Kohlberg concluded that moral is "the realm of abstract universal principles formulated by disembodied subjects. . . . Since the Enlightenment they [men and women] have been taught that morality is defined as the realm of abstract principle, that it eschews the particular, the contingent, and the emotional."[5] Kohlberg concluded that women's level of what is ethically normal is less than what that level is in men.[6] Consequently, Kohlberg agreed with Freud's assertion that, "more often influenced in their judgments by their feeling, women show less sense of justice than men."[7]

---

2. Shima Rostami, *Ethics of Care in Action: A Review After Its 30 Years of Establishment*, 6 J. Ed. Leadership in Action (2019) (quoting Lars Stoltzfus-Brown, PhD candidate, in *Feminist Ethics of Care Literature Review* published in 2018), https://www.lindenwood.edu/academics/beyond-the-classroom/publications/journal-of-educational-leadership-in-action/all-issues/volume-6-issue-1/ethics-of-care-in-action/.

3. Sigmund Freud, Some Psychical Consequences of the Anatomical Distinction Between the Sexes XIX 257–58 (1925).

4. Carol Gilligan, In a Different Voice: Psychological Theory and Women's Development 17 (1982).

5. Susan J. Hekman, Moral Voices, Moral Selves: Carol Gilligan and Feminist Moral Theory 101 (1995).

6. Rostami, *supra* note 2.

7. Freud, *supra* note 3, at 257–58 (1925).

Gilligan pointed out that "what Kohlberg identified as problems in women were in fact problems in the framework of interpretation" by men.[8]

Furthermore, it should be noted that Kohlberg used "white, middle to upper class, predominantly Protestant males, who were in good educational systems" as the sample for his study.[9] Kohlberg's small and biased sample population raised the question whether his results could be accurately expanded to all human beings. In contrast, Gilligan used a diverse and broader sample population that was "characterized not by gender but theme."[10] Gilligan additionally clarified that, in her theory, "no claims are made about the origins of the differences described or their distribution in a wider population, across cultures, or through time."[11] She cleared her study from becoming another analysis of the influence of gender. In fact, as a woman, Gilligan's efforts to show that justice was a human issue beyond gender echoed the voices of so many women all around the world who had been ignored for a long time because "gender is embedded in the images, ideas, and language of a society and is used as a means to divide up work, allocate resources, and distribute power."[12] In other words, Gilligan was "arguing that the patriarchy had deliberately set out to ignore the voices of women and to establish parameters that stifled people's deepest feelings."[13]

In general, to better understand Gilligan's voice not as an individual but also in the context of a social movement, one should consider the social framework in which her voice arose. In fact, in the late 1980s and 1990s, "a religious war [was] going on in our country for the soul of America,"[14] and several issues, including women's rights, fed a liberal movement in American society. Particularly, "the decade of the 1990s was noted for the ascendance of cultural issues to the forefront of American politics and a growing political division between those that hold traditional versus progressive moral values."[15] To that effect, "by naming

8. Carol Gilligan, Ethics of Care 13 (Monograph No. 30, Fundació Víctor Grífols i Lucas 2013).

9. Julia T. Wood, *Gender and the Development of Self: Inclusive Pedagogy in Interpersonal Communication*, 15 Women's Stud. in Comm. 1–24 (1992).

10. Gilligan, *supra* note 4, at 2.

11. *Id.*

12. Diana Kendall, Sociology in Our Times: The Essentials 324 (7th ed. 2008).

13. Victoria Camps, *Introduction*, *in* Gilligan, *supra* note 8, at 7.

14. James A. Henretta, America: A Concise History 2, 919 (6th ed. 2016).

15. Karen M. Kaufmann, *Culture Wars, Secular Realignment, and the Gender Gap in Party Identification*, 24 Pol. Behav. 283 (2002).

and changing the voice of psychological and moral theory, *In a Different Voice* [by Gilligan] shifted the framework, and with this shift, the different voice no longer sounds different. It is, simply, a human voice."[16]

In Iran, previously known as Persia, similarly, it has been women's everyday struggle to find their places and amplify their voices. Persian women have had a long history of fighting for justice and finding their places to help shape the domestic and international agenda. Legends and stories have been told, generation after generation, to exhibit Persian-Iranian women's power and capability of having a place at the table to make decisions while being just. Sometimes, their voices got lost, deliberately or out of ignorance; however, Iranian women, living in the heart of the influential Persian Empire, have played key roles in promoting justice and advocating for social change for their country and the world. History recorded that Iranian "women held positions as managers and supervisors, merchants, soldiers, court clerks, priestesses as well as working as laborers, artisans, and entertainers."[17]

The following is a very brief summary of women's rights and voting status in two eras of the contemporary time in Iran—the Qajar era and the Constitutional Revolution in Iran from 1850 until 1925, and the Pahlavi era from 1925 until the Islamic Revolution of 1979.

The Qajar Era and the Constitutional Revolution in Iran (1850–1925)

Around the mid-19th century, Iran, known as Persia, had lost its independence through catastrophic military events and wars.[18] The colonial lords were taking over the country. Britain needed Iran in order to keep its control over India. Russia was very interested in keeping its political control over Iran, since the country was the Russians' gate to many other neighboring countries in the region. On the other hand, Iran's government at the time, the Qajar, "bled the country dry by selling lands, concessions, privileges, and even peasants into slavery [while] squandering the revenues on palaces, luxuries, pensions, presents, and foreign trips."[19]

---

16. GILLIGAN, *supra* note 8, at 13.

17. Joshua J. Mark, *Twelve Great Women of Ancient Persia*, BREWMINATE (Feb. 2, 2020), https://brewminate.com/twelve-great-women-of-ancient-persia/.

18. HAMIDEH SEDGHI, WOMEN AND POLITICS IN IRAN: VEILING, UNVEILING, AND REVEILING 40 (2007) (quoting Amin Banani in THE MODERNIZATION OF IRAN: 1921–1941 (1984)).

19. AMIN BANANI, THE MODERNIZATION OF IRAN: 1921–1941 3 (1984).

However, Iranians did not tolerate the humiliation of foreigners intervening in their internal politics; they started and mobilized various protests, including the Tobacco Protest of 1891–1892. Women, particularly, played a critical role in this protest and exhibited their hidden or secret power.

This period started with women acquiring the right to equality and the elimination of oppression. In various movements, incidents, and campaigns during this time, Iranian women were incredibly active in various capacities, and they did not fear for their lives. In this period, women in Iran "had potential and hidden power."[20] In fact, women exercised "the policy of secret presence" and, "[t]hus, as mothers, sisters, or wives of the king, they exercised influence over the royal power indirectly."[21]

An example of women's "secret" power and influence is evident in the Tobacco Protest, which was "against the granting of a monopoly over the production, sale, and export of all of Iran's tobacco to the British."[22] When the concession "threatened the profits of domestic businesses, massive protests began against the government and the concession."[23] Various groups in the community joined the protesters. In fact, religious scholars were at the heart of these protests, which mobilized the community, among them ordinary citizens, reformist groups, and women, against the government. Homeira Ranjbar Omrani described the protest as a "prominent move" for women:

> Following the opposition of the clergy and Mirza Hassan Shirazi's fatwa [religious order] banning tobacco smoking, protests became so widespread that women of the Shah's [King's] household avoided smoking of tobacco. They also objected to the king and the tobacco deal and broke all bubbles [hookahs] in the royal household. Spread opposition led Nasseraddin Shah [King] command Mirza Hassan Ashtiani to smoke bubble before the eyes of people or exit from Tehran. Thus, Mirza took the decision to leave Tehran. This brought a great wave of population into the streets, a large part of it included women.[24]

---

20. Homeira Ranjbar Omrani, *An Overview of the Role of Women in the Constitutional Revolution*, IRAN REV. (Mar. 6, 2012), http://www.iranreview.org/content/Documents/An_Overview_of_the_Role_of_Women_in_the_Constitutional_Revolution.htm.

21. *Id.*

22. SEDGHI, *supra* note 18, at 40–41.

23. *Id.*

24. Ranjbar Omrani, *supra* note 20.

Shortly after the Tobacco Protest, through the bread shortage crisis in the Qajar era, women continued participating in the riots and the resistance overall. It is reported that "Zinat Pasha, a woman from the city of Tabriz, who is described as passionate, brave and enlightened" directed a group of veiled armed women toward the market.[25] Later, during the Constitutional Revolution, women started to raise their voices louder and to ask not only for an Iran free from foreigners manipulating their governors but also for a constitution and education. To do so, women established secret and private societies and organizations that later became public; continued participating in the riots; boycotted imported fabrics; donated some of their belongings, including their jewelry, to the constitutional movement; and some joined the movement as armed groups. Additionally, due to religious and cultural expectations concerning women's appearance in public, to have special coverage, some women who joined the armed groups wore men's clothing and participated in combat. On this note, "bodies of twenty women wearing men's clothes were found among the fallen."[26]

It is important to remember that, in those days, there were no "social media" platforms as we have today. People were not able to learn about what was going on in other parts of the world in a matter of seconds; rather, they depended on information from travelers, fellow visitors, or scholars studying abroad. Thus, as Iranian intellectuals started traveling more frequently to European capitals in the mid-19th century, they brought home ideas about liberty and individual autonomy. The international movement calling for equal rights for women, especially in respect of political participation and enfranchisement, was one such concept.[27] Coming from educated scholars, the belief that women should have the right to vote merged with movements that Iranian women had already started in the prior 50 years, unifying these different voices together for women's enfranchisement, which was clearly reflected in the Constitutional Revolution. In other words, women's participation in various movements, protests, and riots at different levels in the past decades made the ground ready for them to acquire the right to vote officially.

The Constitutional Revolution in Iran from 1905 to 1911 was the starting point of an official conversation to define Iranian women's role

25. SEDGHI, *supra* note 18, at 41.

26. LOIS BECK & GUITY NASHAT, WOMEN IN IRAN FROM 1800 TO THE ISLAMIC REPUBLIC 89 (2004) (citing AHMAD KASRAVI, TRAIKH-E MASHRUTIYAT-E IRAN [HISTORY OF THE IRAN CONSTITUTION] 698 (1970)).

27. Arzoo Osanloo, *Lessons from the Suffrage Movement in Iran*, 129 YALE L.J. 496, 499 (2020).

in society. Debates started off unconcerned about women's right to vote; rather, debates discussed women's social activities, as it was more a conversation about shifting gender roles in the society. Consideration of the right to vote for women was not a focus of the Constitutional Revolution. Instead, these movements and debates not only made the ground ready for Iranian women to engage in political actions but also created an enabling environment, including preparing people's thinking and attitudes to accept women's participation in political decision-making.

The Pahlavi Era to the Islamic Revolution (1925–1979)

In 1925, Reza Khan abolished the Qajar empire, founded the Pahlavi empire, and became the shah. Some of Reza Khan's actions might appear as good, constructive moves. For example, legal reforms improved women's marital rights:

> The Majles [Parliament] approved a new civil code that granted women the right to ask for divorce under certain conditions. The legal age for marriage for girls was increased [raised] to 15. Reza Shah ordered his minister of education to establish the Kanoun-e Banovan (Women's Center), headed by Shams, Reza Shah's daughter, and Hajar Tarbiyat.[28]

Nevertheless, some described his time as "oppression, corruption, taxation, lack of authenticity," causing more damage to the country than good.[29] According to some scholars, "autocracy meant the defeat of women's independent activities and the creation of a new feminism under state auspices."[30] Reza Shah's order for the unveiling of women in 1935 increased the isolation of some previously publicly and politically active women. For example, there were about 3,470 female students in Iran in 1925 at the beginning of Reza Shah's time; however, only 2,600 women participated in the university in 1935 right after the compulsory unveiling

28. Muhammad Sahimi, *Iranian Women and the Struggle for Democracy*, PBS Frontline (Apr. 15, 2010 20:25), https://www.pbs.org/wgbh/pages/frontline/tehranbureau/2010/04/iranian-women-and-the-struggle-for-democracy-i-the-pre-revolution-era.html.

29. Ervand Abrahamian, History of Modern Iran 94 (2018).

30. Sedghi, *supra* note 18, at 18.

began.[31] Immediately after Reza Shah's removal from office, the number of female students in higher education increased to more than 5,800.[32]

During Reza Shah's reign, feminism struggled:

> Following World War I, repression had largely destroyed an incipient Iranian feminism. Although Doulatabadi and a few other women had introduced feminism, there was no light at the end of the tunnel. Reza Shah Pahlavi replaced independent women's movement with "state feminism" and coercively enforced unveiling. Women had spoken out against imperialism, the state, and patriarchy. The renewal of free feminist debate and activity would wait until the near disappearance of the state after the abdication of Reza Shah Pahlavi in 1941.[33]

After Reza Shah's son, Shah Mohammad Reza Pahlavi, came into office, women who were mainly suppressed in Reza Shah's time restarted their political activities more publicly, and they began setting up women's organizations again with branches in the main cities all around the country. In the municipal councils in 1952, Dr. Mosaddegh, the 35th prime minister of Iran, granted women not only the right to vote but also equal rights with men.[34] This package included maternity leave, to go along with plural benefits and plural disability allowances to women.[35] However, "the CIA-MI6 coup of 1953 that overthrew Dr. Mosaddegh's government again put a temporary stop to the gains that women were making."[36]

Finally, after going through a series of movements and activities, in 1963, Shah Mohammad Reza Pahlavi granted women a full right to vote, like Iranian men, in all elections.[37] This decision was rejected by Ayatollah Ruhollah Khomeini, the founder of the Islamic Revolution of Iran.[38] However, roughly 16 years later, in 1979, the same cleric not only approved the right to vote for women but also announced that women need to run for various official seats, including city councils, parliaments, and other offices.

31. Sahimi, *supra* note 28.
32. *Id.*
33. SEDGHI, *supra* note 18, at 58.
34. Sahimi, *supra* note 28.
35. *Id.*
36. *Id.*
37. *Id.*
38. *Id.*

One may ask why Iranian women joined the Islamic Revolution of 1979 against Shah Mohammad Reza Pahlavi, even though he granted them the right to vote and some other rights to be equal to men's rights.

On this note, professor Muhammad Sahimi observes that women felt their rights were ineffective and unequal because they lacked meaningful political inclusion and participation:

> The answer is simple. Many intellectual women considered their political advances as bogus. The Shah's absolute dictatorial rule had made it impossible for intellectuals, political dissidents, and opposition groups to be openly active. There was no free press, no democratic elections, no true opposition, and heavy-handed censorship of all media and publications. So, the fact that there were, for example, 22 female Majles [Parliament] deputies and two female senators in 1978—all of them Shah loyalists—impressed few women. Aside from the tightly controlled, officially sanctioned outlets, women had no forum in which to express their concerns, let alone engage freely in political activity.[39]

Despite their remarkable educational achievement after the Islamic Revolution of 1979, Iranian women still have one of the lowest levels of representation in parliament in the world—only 5.6 percent, or 16 seats out of 285 total, as of May 2020.[40] More recently, on May 25, 2021, Iran approved seven men from a total of 592 candidates, only 40 of whom were women, for the June 18 presidential election; all 40 women candidates were disqualified by the Guardian Council, a body with several duties, including vetting election candidates.[41] Many women have stepped forward and volunteered for the presidential position under the Islamic Republic. However, the Guardian Council has rejected and disqualified all women for the past 40 years, including the recent elections in 2021. As mentioned earlier, this chapter does not address Iranian women's status rights in the contemporary era, as it requires further in-depth discussions.

39. *Id.*

40. *Islamic Parliament of Iran*, Inter-Parliamentary Union, https://data.ipu.org/content/iran-islamic-republic (last visited June 1, 2021).

41. *See* Garrett Nada & Andrew Hanna, *Presidential Election 2021: Candidates*, U.S. Institute of Peace, The Iran Primer (May 26, 2021) (updated June 16, 2020), https://iranprimer.usip.org/index.php/blog/2021/may/26/presidential-election-candidates.

Conclusion

Carol Gilligan recognized the era of culture wars in America as a moral injury that needed to be healed. She indicated that the culture wars are a battle between democracy and patriarchy when, "[t]he Love Laws are a mainstay of patriarchy. The ethic of care in its concern with voice and relationships is the ethic of love and of democratic citizenship. It is also the ethic of resistance to moral injury."[42] As it is defined, moral injury "consists of the destruction of trust and the loss of the capacity to love."[43] What is still missing in the world is to find a solution to cure the moral injury of women. This injury has developed over time by women being ignored and unheard across various cultures only because they are women.

Suppression of women has been supported by various lines of thought, including the claim that they "care too much," thereby limiting women's capacity to be just and to make fair decisions on their own. However, what has been considered as a negative feature in women, caring, is actually a strong positive feature in them as human beings since "justice must be complemented by care."[44]

Lastly, women's culture wars should be considered a universal movement in that, with their different voices, veiled or unveiled, secular or religious, women have been singing the same melody across the ages. To be American or Iranian, women and their movements, including their efforts to get the right to vote, have not been left out of this universal movement. More importantly, it is the author's hope that women's rights movements, such as #metoo, will grow to speak up about all forms of discrimination against women.

---

42. GILLIGAN, *supra* note 8, at 14.
43. Camps, *supra* note 13, at 9.
44. *Id.* at 8.

7

Japan: Pushback against Pushbacks—Why We Need More Women in Parliament in Japan

Hayashi Yoko[1]

Let me first begin by congratulating the United States on the 100th anniversary of the passage of the 19th Amendment to the U.S. Constitution in 2020.

The centennial anniversary became a year when protests to address racial and social injustices in the United States became a global phenomenon. Solidarity to end discrimination, racism, poverty, and inequalities spread throughout the world in 2020, including within my country, Japan. The widespread political and social protests are a reminder that history has always been changed not by elite politicians but by people who have collectively or individually expressed their beliefs through concrete actions. Now, as we emerge from the pandemic, we have not just an opportunity but also an obligation to overcome historical inequities and discrimination and to infuse our future with inclusion, diversity, and equality.

Women's Suffrage in Japan

Women in Japan first exercised their right to vote in April 1946, eight months after Japan's surrender resulting in the end of World War II. Thirty-nine women were elected to the House of Representatives (the lower house) representing 8.4 percent of the total membership, which in

1. Hayashi Yoko is a lawyer and former chair of the United Nations Committee on the Elimination of Discrimination Against Women (CEDAW).

the 1940s was recorded as one of the highest percentages of women represented in a parliament in the world. The women parliamentarians participated in the adoption of the new constitution, which contains articles prohibiting discrimination based on sex (Article 14) and guaranteeing the equality of both sexes in marriage and family (Article 24), together with the renunciation of war (Article 9).

The most prominent activist in the women's suffrage movement in Japan was Ichikawa Fusae, who joined the New Women's Association (NWA) founded by Hiratsuka Raichō in 1919. NWA was the first women's civic organization in modern Japan. Its initial mandate was to repeal a provision in the Police Act prohibiting women from attending political meetings. Ichikawa lived in the United States between 1921 and 1923, immediately after the 19th Amendment to the U.S. Constitution was passed. Thanks to her detailed memoir, we may learn how she was influenced by the great American women whom she met, including Alice Paul, a leader of the National Women's Party, and Jeannette Rankin, the first woman elected to the U.S. Congress. In the prewar period in Japan, the House of Representatives (the lower house) adopted the women's suffrage bill in 1930, but the bill was vetoed by the House of Peers (the upper house).

One can easily imagine that the main contributing factor that realized women's suffrage in Japan was the instruction to the government from the General Headquarters of the Allied Forces, which occupied the country from 1945 to 1952. However, what Ichikawa, who herself became a member of the House of Councilors (the upper house) in 1953, emphasized was that women's right to vote in Japan was not merely a "gift" from Douglas MacArthur, but was an outcome of the domestic women's movement that continued from the prewar period. Ichikawa always stressed that women in Japan gained their rights with their own hands.

Ichikawa played a critical role in guiding the reluctant Japanese government to ratify the Convention on the Elimination of All Forms of Discrimination Against Women (CEDAW) in 1985.[2] When she passed away in 1981, the text of the CEDAW Convention was placed inside her coffin to pay homage to her life dedicated to promoting the human rights of women.

Japan enjoyed rapid economic growth during the postwar decades; however, such growth was achieved by government policies that reinforced gender stereotypes in every sphere of society, including the workplace, family, and communities.

2. *See* Convention on the Elimination of All Forms of Discrimination Against Women, Dec. 18, 1979, 1249 U.N.T.S. 13 (entered into force Sept. 3, 1981).

Expanding Women's Representation in Parliament

At the present time, the level of Japanese women's participation in politics is regrettably low. According to the gender statistics of the Inter-Parliamentary Union (IPU), Japan ranks 164th out of 193 countries in the percentage of women represented in the lower house, at only 9.9 percent, and 43rd out of 81 countries for the upper house representation, at only 23.0 percent, as of June 2021.[3] A political scientist has described this phenomenon as "democracy without women." Yet, what kind of "democracy" can exist without proportionate representation of half of its national population?

The Committee on the Elimination of Discrimination Against Women (CEDAW Committee) has repeatedly recommended that Japan introduce temporary special measures (affirmative or positive action) to accelerate the change.[4] Being inspired by the CEDAW Committee's recommendation, a nonpartisan women's group, named the Association for the Promotion of Quotas, was formed in 2012. The group began lobbying political parties to enact a new law on gender quotas for candidates for public office. In 2018, after a number of failed attempts in the parliamentary sessions, the Act on the Promotion of Gender Equality in the Political Field (commonly known as the Gender Parity Law in Public Office) was finally adopted by consensus.[5] Because of compromises that had to be made during a period in which the draft bill was pending, the enacted act is very lenient and without any sanctions. Article 4 provides that political organizations are to endeavor to voluntarily work on the promotion of gender equality, including setting a goal for the number of male and female candidates. Nevertheless, the Gender Parity Law in Public Office has produced some notable changes subsequently, no matter how modest, as described next.

In 2019, a series of elections for local assemblies and a national election for the upper house were held. For the first time, female local assembly members attained more than 30 percent of the seats in Tokyo's 23 municipalities,[6] and the percentage of women candidates for the upper

3. *Monthly Ranking of Women in National Parliaments*, INTER-PARLIAMENTARY UNION, https://data.ipu.org/women-ranking (last updated June 1, 2021).

4. *See* United Nations, Comm. on the Elimination of Discrimination Against Women, Concluding Observations on the Combined Seventh and Eighth Periodic Reports of Japan, U.N. Doc. CEDAW/C/JPN/7-8 (Mar. 7, 2016).

5. Seiji Bun'ya ni Okeru Danjo Kyōdō Sankaku no Suishin ni Kansuru Hōritsu [Act on the Promotion of Gender Equality in the Political Field], Law No. 28 of 2018 (Japanese).

6. Shin Yasutaka, *Record No. of Female City Mayors, Assembly Members Elected in Japan's Unified Local Polls*, THE MAINICHI, Apr. 22, 2019.

house election set the highest record in the country's history at 28.1 percent.[7] Moreover, we have witnessed important positive changes in two areas: in the mass media and within political parties.

Mainstream media began reporting about the root causes of women's underrepresentation in politics, such as pervasive gender stereotyping, sexual harassment against female politicians and candidates, and insufficient work and family life balance in the parliament. Stories of various women candidates, too, were frequently reported during the campaign, covering, for example, what motivated women to become politicians, how they prepared and organized campaigns, and how things could be compatible with their private lives.

Another positive change took place within political parties. Some parties had not even tracked statistics on the percentage of women parliamentarians representing their own parties in national and local assemblies, but it is fair to say that they have now become more serious in pursuing gender parity as a goal in candidature.

Strengthening Women's Rights Worldwide

We live in an era when democracy is challenged not only by authoritarian regimes but also by some political leaders in so-called free states. At the United Nations, we are hearing the emergence of voices representing some of the Member States that intentionally diminish the centrality of human rights in the activities of the organization. Above all, pushbacks against women's rights are becoming intensified in various parts of the world in recent years, especially in areas pertaining to their reproductive and sexual health rights. We have more legitimacy than any time in the past to press for more women in the parliament because democracy will be reinforced by participation of people with diversified backgrounds.

Finally, as a former chairperson of the CEDAW Committee, I do hope that the United States will ratify the CEDAW Convention in the very near future. There is no doubt that the tradition of law in the United States will give added value to the work of CEDAW if the U.S. government, experts, and nongovernmental organizations (NGOs) may participate in and contribute to the dialogues taking place in CEDAW. To pushback against pushbacks, the necessity of strengthening this legally binding, universal instrument cannot be emphasized enough.

7. Hironori Takechi & Tetsuya Kageyama, *Record Ratio of Women Running in Japan Upper House Race, but Inclusion Efforts Uneven*, THE MAINICHI, July 5, 2019.

8

Kenya: Reflections on Preventing Sexual and Gender-Based Election Violence

Rachel Irura[1]

The first and last opportunity I had to vote in the Kenyan elections was in December 2007. I will provide some context to this. I left Kenya after completing my high school studies in 1995 at the age of 18 and therefore missed the next election cycle. I then studied for my undergraduate law degree in Roma, Lesotho, and thereafter for my graduate law degree in human rights in Pretoria, South Africa, on a full scholarship. I did an internship focused on women's rights issues in Accra, Ghana, and worked briefly for an umbrella body of civil society organizations in Johannesburg, South Africa. I then proceeded to work as a legal assistant for the Special Court for Sierra Leone, in Freetown, Sierra Leone, and thereafter in the Human Rights and Protection Section for the UN Mission in Liberia. This all then culminated in a move to The Hague, the Netherlands, to work as a court officer in the trial of Charles Taylor, the former president of Liberia who was convicted for war crimes, and thereafter for the Special Tribunal for Lebanon as a legal officer in court management services. In total, I spent 12.5 years working in The Hague. I then worked in Kigali, Rwanda, where I double-hatted as the head of the office and the head of the Witness Support and Protection Unit. I presently work in Arusha in the latter role. While these career moves have been good for my career, they have left me in the unfortunate position of only having voted once in my country of birth, Kenya. Unfortunately, for Kenyans who live in the diaspora, the right to vote, though enshrined in the Constitution of Kenya, remains a mirage.

1. Rachel Irura is the head of the Witness Support and Protection Unit at the United Nations International Residual Mechanism for Criminal Tribunals. The views expressed are the author's personal views.

Let me draw a picture of the climate in Kenya when I first had the opportunity to exercise this right. I was extremely excited because, for once, my annual leave and annual visit to Kenya coincided with the 2007 Kenyan elections. This was an alignment that had eluded me for years due to the pursuit of education and career. In 2007, there had been highly active electioneering—as usual on tribal lines. But for once, the air was marked with a lot of tension, as two candidates from opposing tribes were running for president. The campaigns had been fraught with violence, as the Kikuyu and Luo tribes galvanized their masses to ensure their candidate won. Voting in Kenya unfortunately remains an ethnic issue. It is also dominated by patriarchy, as invariably all the parliamentary and presidential candidates tend to be male. The few women candidates are either nominated members of parliament or have borne the brunt of criticism and great personal expense to their families, as well as social and other stigmas to win a ticket to parliament.

Why Empowering Rural Women Matters

I digress briefly to recount my earliest memories of elections in Kenya. When I was growing up, every school holiday, since I was 6 to 14 years old, my parents would dispatch us to stay with my grandmother for about a month in the village, two hours' drive from Nairobi. There were three school terms, and we would therefore spend three months in the village. I vividly remember the election campaigns as I lived them through the eyes of the village women. This was a time filled with song and dance as each parliamentarian tried to outdo the other. Lorries filled with singing youth and women would pass by the road near my grandfather's farm. Handouts of money and basic foodstuffs were the order of the day as each candidate "solicited" for voters. Women invariably were the target. They were given printed cloth, or *lesos* in Kiswahili, to wrap around their waists with the candidate's picture and slogan, as well as t-shirts with the same political branding. At the time, it was a lot of fun to watch, as the air buzzed with excitement. My grandmother, too, would often join in these frays and sometimes take us with her. For a child, it was an exciting time.

Today, I look back and wonder whether this was not unduly influencing women voters. Could one not even call it buying their votes with handouts? This is not a rhetorical question, because of course it was manipulation of the highest level. These were village women without an education—my grandmother who is in her late nineties and still alive today is illiterate. Poverty was and remains rife in the village, and therefore sugar, milk, and bread meant a lot to these women. They were up for the highest bidder. They sadly never knew the power of their vote.

Civic education has changed the election landscape, but a lot remains the same. The votes of women are usually purchased for a few thousand Kenyan shillings. Women continue to be manipulated out of their votes by a highly patriarchal society. Every election cycle, the candidates may change, but the outcome of the "democratic process" remains the same. The roads have not been built. The health facilities lack basic amenities. The primary and secondary school structures are falling apart due to lack of maintenance. A few people continue to enrich themselves out of the public coffers at the expense of the *mwananchi*—ordinary citizen in Kiswahili.

This scourge is felt by all, but women and children are the most affected. Each year, thousands of women die during labor because of poor maternal health facilities and lack of prenatal and antenatal care. I had my daughter in a hospital in the Netherlands, and I never forget, even for a minute, how fortunate and privileged I am. Many of my counterparts, fellow women in Kenya, are not so fortunate. There are very well-staffed and equipped hospitals in the capital cities, but they remain the respite of a privileged few.

The education of the girl child continues to be eroded, as many girls fall prey to early pregnancy and drop out of school due to early marriages. Female genital mutilation continues to haunt some societies in Kenya. In a society dominated by patriarchy, women continue to be treated as second-class citizens. This is true unfortunately even for Kenya, which has many emancipated and educated women and is viewed as a bastion of women's empowerment in Africa. It is the land of activists, such as the late Wangari Maathai, an environmentalist, the first woman in Kenya to receive a PhD, and the first African woman to receive the Nobel Peace Prize in 2004. In her book *Taking Root*, she outlines that activism cost her—her personal life. The man she loved and married divorced her because she was too emancipated, and her ideals were too high for an African woman. She was not conformist enough. The only thing that she retained was her husband's surname because it was on her education certificates. When he demanded she give up his surname as part of the divorce, she inserted an additional "a" into Mathai to create Maathai as her new legal surname.

This type of patriarchal attitude holds true in Kenya even today; the term "independent woman" is tossed about like a curse. I draw these parallels because it grieves me deeply when women in Kenya trade their rights and power at the ballot box to a male candidate offering them money and basic supplies, sometimes little more than a kilogram of sugar or maize flour. It simply boils down to a meal for their family for one night. That is how cheaply a woman in Kenya is coerced to give up her right to vote. The only difference between the past and today is, at least then, there was no politically motivated violence.

Voting as a Woman in the 2007 Kenyan Elections

On one misty morning in December 2007, I arose early to exercise my right to universal adult suffrage, my right to vote in the presidential and parliamentary elections. I voted for the candidate of my choice. I woke up at dawn and stood in line with thousands of other Kenyans who wanted to change the political discourse of the country. What followed was a total nightmare. It all began when the results from the presidential elections began filtering onto our television screens. I went to sleep late at night and left the results tilted in the favor of one candidate. I woke up the next morning and found that they had now shifted in favor of the other candidate. That was when all mayhem broke loose.

The worst post-election violence to ever hit Kenya occurred. Thousands lost their lives. The country burst into flames, literally. It was reminiscent of the genocide against the Tutsi in Rwanda, as tribe descended upon tribe based on ethnicity. The footage from the scenes was chilling. I could hear gunshots from my parents' house. One's ethnic identity became their saving grace. I was in Kenya waiting to return to the Netherlands after my annual leave, and I was trapped—the airport was surrounded by protestors, and exit was not possible. I received calls from my office in the Netherlands about whether I wished to be evacuated. My response was a resounding: "No!" At least I was with my family members who were equally terrified, and I did not want to be evacuated only because I was a staff member of a UN-affiliated court.

Post-Election Sexual and Gender-Based Violence

Not ironically, the persons most affected by the post-election violence were women. They paid with their lives for having exercised their hard-won right to vote. Women were the victims of sexual and gender-based violence, such as rape. Many women whose votes opposed those of their husbands were victims of domestic violence, divorce, or, in the worst scenario, death. In ethnically motivated violence, women and children were set ablaze in a church where they were sheltering. A friend recounted to me how her aunt escaped the violence because a friendly neighbor warned her husband to take his wife away if he wished her to live, as she was from a different tribe. Yet another family friend recounted to me how she and her children holed themselves up, prayed as they waited for the violence to end, and hoped that their neighbors who were from a different tribe and had been their good friends would not turn on them. Many women were displaced, assaulted, and hacked to death—for tribal affiliations. A question would be posed, and, if you did not answer in your tribal language—the "right tribal language"—you would perish. This was not the Kenya I grew up in, where my grandmother and her peers sang songs during the electioneering period. This was a Kenya where henceforth announcing elections would be a death knell.

The culmination of the 2007 elections was a quick swearing-in ceremony for one of the candidates who then became Kenya's president-elect. In the meantime, I managed to return to The Hague when the furor had died down a bit. From there, I watched the news helplessly as the mayhem and destruction continued. Lawlessness had become the order of the day, and the police responded with brutal force. It quickly became apparent that, without the intervention of the international community, Kenya would be the genesis of another Rwanda, to which the world had sworn "never again." Comparisons of this nature were already being drawn in the media.

The African Union intervened under the ambit of former UN secretary-general Kofi Annan to restore peace to the country. Subsequently, the International Criminal Court (ICC) indicted six persons for the post-election violence. Two of those indicted eventually became the president and deputy president of the Republic of Kenya. The cases ran their course at the ICC and were eventually dismissed for "lack of evidence."[2] When the cases commenced at the ICC, many victims and witnesses, among them women who were affected by the post-election violence, came forward to testify. Unfortunately, to date, most of the victims and witnesses are still grieving because, for them, justice has not been done.

2. Press Release, Columbia Law Sch., Kenya ICC Case Dismissed for Lack of Evidence, Declared a Mistrial (Apr. 5, 2016), https://web.law.columbia.edu/human-rights-institute/news-features/press-releases/kenya-icc-case-dismissed-lack-evidence-declared-mistrial.

Constitutional Right to Vote and Diaspora

The right to vote was granted to all Kenyans when Kenya gained its independence from the United Kingdom on December 12, 1963. The Constitution of Kenya provides that every adult citizen has the right to vote by secret ballot in any election or referendum. The Elections Act accentuates this constitutional right by providing for the legal framework for exercising the right. Article 3 of the act states that "an adult citizen shall exercise the right to vote specified in Article 38(3) of the Constitution in accordance with this Act . . . if the citizen is registered in the Register of Voters."[3] Article 82(1)(c) of the constitution calls for "the continuous registration of citizens as voters."

My grievance and that of other Kenyans living, studying, and working in the diaspora is that they have not been able to actualize their right to vote. Since the new constitution was promulgated in 2010 ushering in this right, our right to vote as diaspora Kenyans living outside of East African countries has not been fully realized. This affects both Kenyan men and women. The excuses have been numerous, from the inability of Kenyan embassies abroad to register voters, to a lack of equipment, to an inability to vote electronically. Kenyans have even requested to go and queue physically at embassies abroad to realize this right, but this has not been made possible. This is reprehensible, because more than 25 African countries allow their nationals abroad to vote at their embassies. To date, Kenya remains an exception. The Kenyan embassy in the Netherlands where I lived and worked was not able to facilitate this right during my period of residence in that country.

The body that governs elections in Kenya, the Independent Electoral and Boundaries Commission (IEBC), uses Article 82(1)(e) "progressive registration of citizens residing outside Kenya, and the progressive realization of their right to vote," to keep the diaspora disenfranchised. "Progressive realization" is a gray area, subject to interpretation that suits whoever holds the keys to diaspora participation. The "progressive realization" phrase leads to the suppression of the right to vote of an estimated three million Kenyans in the diaspora.

Persistent Barriers to Women's Participation in Elections

In the wake of the 2007 elections in Kenya and the aftermath, there have been two more election cycles, each marked by different levels of violence and an increase in ethnic polarization. In 2017, ten years later, the

3. Elections Act (2011, amended) Cap. 7 § 3; *cf.* CONSTITUTION, art. 38(3) (1992).

presidential election almost brought the country to its knees. Although I was not there to witness it, the economic devastation, violence, and ill will it left among Kenyans persist to date. The scenario had different players but an almost similar outcome. The vote was split almost 50–50 in a winner-takes-all type of presidential system.

This time around, an election rerun was ordered by the Supreme Court after a nullification of the previous poll. The candidate who lost galvanized all his supporters to boycott the rerun, all government-run services, and businesses run by a particular tribe. For almost three months, the country was paralyzed by riots and mass protests marked by running battles between the police and protestors. The streets were filled with teargas and military tanks to dispel the rioters. Businesses remained closed, and the economy was paralyzed. The candidate who won continued in power in utter disregard of all this.

Ethnicity became the norm among Kenyans in the country and those in the diaspora. Social media frequented by Kenyans was filled with hate speech and incitement to violence along tribal and ethnic lines. Women's groups and civil society tried to intervene to bring some semblance of sanity to the situation, in vain. There was widespread sexual violence against women and the use of arbitrary force by the police to quell protestors. The government stopped all news outlets in the country from broadcasting the scenes by clamping down on the media. Once again, I watched in horror from The Hague as all these scenes unfolded in the international media, which was not barred from broadcasting. The handshake between the two opposing candidates in January 2018 brought much needed relief and peace, shaky peace, as the two warring factions called their protestors off the streets.

Unfortunately, elections in Kenya for many women have become symbolic of cycles of violence against women, and many live in fear at the thought of a repeat of the past. For women, the police, who are supposed to protect them, became perpetrators of sexual and gender-based violence crimes like rape during the post-election mayhem. They often get away with these crimes due to a culture of impunity that pervades the police force in Kenya.

Activism to Advance Women's Participation as Political Leaders and Peacebuilders

I reminisce about a different time in a different African country when the election process had a different outcome. The scene is set in Liberia, an African country where the voices and the votes of women were able to avert a war and put a female presidential candidate into power. This was the election of Ellen Johnson Sirleaf, as the first female president in Liberia and the first African female president.

After a decade-long war in Liberia, both Christian and Muslim women came together in a call for peace. A peace movement called Women of Liberia Mass Action for Peace was formed. It was organized by social worker Leymah Gbowee. The movement started with praying and singing in a fish market. Leymah Gbowee organized the Christian and Muslim women in Monrovia, Liberia, to pray for peace and to organize nonviolent protests. Dressed in white to symbolize peace, and numbering in the thousands, the women became a political force against violence and against their government. The women demanded for Charles Taylor to step down as president and for peaceful elections to be held in the wake of his departure. They mobilized and voted collectively for presidential candidate Sirleaf.

The collective action of those women culminated in the documentary film "Pray the Devil Back to Hell," which was shown at The Hague Movies that Matter Festival in 2009, with a related panel discussion in which I was invited to participate. It was a great honor for me as one of my fellow panelists was Fatou Bensouda, a deputy prosecutor, and, later, the prosecutor of the International Criminal Court (ICC). I was young and felt empowered to share a table with such an eminent lawyer. My head was in the clouds for days on end after that. The film premiered at the 2008 Tribeca Film Festival, where it won the award for Best Documentary. It had its theatrical release in New York City in November 2008. The title of the film is drawn from Gbowee's statement about Taylor and the rebels, as both sides were supposedly religious. The rebels frequented mosques, while Taylor claimed to be a devout Christian who, according to Gbowee, could "pray the devil out of hell." It was therefore the responsibility of the women in this interfaith coalition to pray the devil (of war) right back to hell. The film has been used as an advocacy tool in post-conflict zones like Sudan, mobilizing African women to petition for peace and security. Both former president Sirleaf and Leymah Gbowee received a Nobel Peace Prize in 2011 for their efforts to advance women's participation in peacebuilding work.

In Kenya, similar activism has gained momentum, where women gather before the elections to discuss how to prevent election-related violence. These women are not politicians, election officials, or campaigners—they are grassroots activists, working with their communities to keep the peace. In the lead-up to the election, they look for early warning signs of violence, inform the police of what they find, map "trouble zones," and host dialogue forums. On the polling day, they monitor polling station lines and urge people to go straight home after voting. This is the activism done by groups like the Kibera Women for Peace and Fairness to Combat Violence and other women's groups in slums like Mathare and Kibera, the largest slum in Kenya. Their activism is aimed at combating post-election violence like that which engulfed the slums in the wake of the 2007 and, more recently, the 2017 elections. Kenya has yet another election looming in 2022. The political activism has once again turned to tribalism and ethnicity, and the trials before the International Criminal Court are a distant memory.

Democracy, Progress, and Peace Require Women's Political Participation

This time I am closer to home, next door in fact, in Arusha, Tanzania. Like many conscientious citizens, I would like to exercise my right to vote. Recalling my first and last experience voting is traumatic for me but even more so for other women who repetitively fall victim to sexual and gender-based violence during each election cycle. I, like many others, hope for a more peaceful and positive outcome in the parliamentary and presidential elections to be held on August 9, 2022. I would like to be optimistic that this time around, my vote and that of other women will count. However, every time I try to focus, the electioneering that fills the television screens does not bode well at all for the peaceful outcome that women in Kenya so desperately desire.

Peaceful elections in Kenya and a climate where women can vote without fearing the repercussions remain my dream for women in Kenya. Realizing this dream requires responsible and ethical leadership at all levels—where politicians take responsibility for their political utterances; where women do not sell their rights to vote for a kilogram of maize or sugar to feed their families; and where Kenyans regard each other as brothers and sisters, regardless of their creed or tribe. Perpetrators of violence against women must be held accountable through thorough investigation and prosecution as a deterrence to others, and women, including those aspiring for political seats and their supporters, must be adequately redressed for any harm suffered in their pursuit of inclusion.[4]

4. *See* Agatha Ndonga & Kelli Muddell, *Ending Gender Violence in Elections: Inclusion of Women in Kenyan Politics and the National Dialogue Process from a*

In addition, Kenya should implement measures to raise awareness about existing social prejudices, customs, and traditions that harm women, and to modify discriminatory policies and all other practices that promote acts of violence against women. This is in line with the spirit of Article 27 of the 2010 Kenyan Constitution, which provides that:

> (1) Every person is equal before the law and has the right to equal protection and equal benefit of the law.
>
> (2) Equality includes the full and equal enjoyment of all rights and fundamental freedoms.
>
> (3) Women and men have the right to equal treatment, including the right to equal opportunities in political, economic, cultural and social spheres.

Transitional Justice Perspective, ICTJ Briefing (Dec. 2019), https://www.ictj.org/sites/default/files/ICTJ_Briefing_Kenya_Women_Inclusion_Web.pdf.

9

United Kingdom: The Legacy and Impact of Women's Suffrage on the Legal Profession

Christina Blacklaws[1]

Women's Access to the Legal Profession

In the United Kingdom, the fight for women's suffrage was inextricably linked to the contemporaneous campaign for the right to be able to practice law. Then, as now, women realized that laws made by parliament and interpreted by the courts had the potential to adversely impact women's rights. Knowledge of the law and access to the legal profession and to legal practice were as essential as the right to vote to ensure women's rights were (and are) protected and promoted.

In 1918, in the United Kingdom, some women were granted the right to vote in the Representation of the People Act 1918. For the first time, approximately 8.4 million women were enfranchised. This represented a great victory for the women's movement. Many of those who had struggled for women's suffrage were also active in campaigning for women's access to the legal profession. Some names will be familiar—even to an international audience—such as Emmeline and Christabel Pankhurst and Millicent Garrett Fawcett, but others less so.

1. Christina Blacklaws is an activist, feminist, speaker, chair of UK government panels, an NED and advisor to international law firms and businesses, and former president of the Law Society of England and Wales. Please email me at christina@blacklawsconsulting.com if you would like to receive soft copies of the toolkits and reports.

One of those who deserves to be celebrated is Gwyneth Marjory Bebb (1889–1921). Bebb was awarded a first-class honors degree in jurisprudence from the University of Oxford—the first woman ever to do so. She applied for permission to sit the Law Society's preliminary examination and was rejected.

Undeterred, Bebb issued proceedings against the Law Society seeking a declaration that she was a "person" within the meaning of the Solicitors Act 1843. She failed in the High Court and then appealed to the Court of Appeal, which rejected her appeal, concluding that women were not "persons" for the purposes of the Solicitors Act and the Law Society could not be compelled to admit Bebb.

She (and others) continued the campaign through the parliament, and, on December 23, 1919, the Sex Disqualification (Removal) Act was passed. In January 1920, Bebb was finally admitted as a student member of Lincoln's Inn. Tragically, she was never called to the bar, as she died in childbirth in 1921 at the age of just 31.

Gwyneth Bebb was a great inspiration for me and many other women who wanted to mark and celebrate the centenaries of (some) women's suffrage and the enablement of women to enter our profession.

I was elected to the position of deputy vice president of the Law Society of England and Wales in July 2016. Our rules mean that you succeed to vice president and then on to president, so I knew I had a three-year term to make a positive difference. I was only the fifth female president out of 174, and, having been a lifelong campaigner for equal opportunities, I wanted to focus on women in the law.

As I started my research, it became clear to me that the problem in the United Kingdom did not relate to women not entering the profession. Women had represented more than 60 percent of newly qualified solicitors for around 15 years and more than half for nearly 30 years.

However, the real issue related to women reaching the higher echelons in the law—becoming a partner in a law firm (28 percent), being appointed a Queen's Counsel (13 percent), and reaching the upper levels of the judiciary (for some positions 0 percent). The figures for these were pitifully low despite decades of a predominantly female talent pipeline.

Together, with the engagement and cooperation of around 15,000 men and women across the globe, through 2018 to 2019, we conducted research to discover what the barriers were to women progressing and what needed to be done to address these barriers.

With the support of the International Bar Association Women Lawyers' Interest Group and LexisNexis, nearly 8,000 people around the world completed our "Women in Law Survey," the largest ever undertaken.

We identified the key barriers to progression:

- 52 percent of respondents saw unconscious and conscious bias as the main barrier;
- 49 percent recognized an unacceptable work/life balance demanded to reach senior levels as a major concern;
- 46 percent were concerned that the law was "male shaped" with traditional networks/route to promotion being male orientated; and
- 60 percent were aware of a gender or equal pay gap issue in their firm or business.[2]

We used these insights to inform our roundtables. In 2019, we completed more than 250 across five continents, in 18 jurisdictions, and involving around 5,000 women and men in the profession.

We created specific toolkits—one for women and one for men—to focus on the primary issues and solutions and to encourage everyone to become activists for gender equality in their organizations and communities.

We grouped our findings into three insight reports: one from the domestic women's roundtables, another from our "Male Champions for Change," and, third, our findings from the international community.

Overwhelmingly, we found that, at every stage of a woman's career, there are barriers preventing her from fulfilling her potential. With a few exceptions, women lawyers still do not uniformly occupy leadership roles commensurate with their wishes, qualifications, experience, and numbers.

Influencing for Impact

In addition to the insights from the survey, we launched our *Influencing for Impact* report on International Women's Day in 2019, which covered the main findings from the women's roundtables in England and Wales.[3] Some of the key themes included the following:

- Not fitting into the traditional image of a business leader—and how the archetypal image of what it takes to lead favors

2. Law Society of England & Wales, Influencing for Impact: The Need for Gender Equality in the Legal Profession (2019), https://www.lawsociety.org.uk/topics/research/women-in-leadership-in-the-law-report-need-for-gender-equality.
3. *Id.*

characteristics that are traditionally male while feminine traits are undervalued or seen negatively.

- Lack of representation. There is a strong desire among women to see people in leadership who are "like me"—people who they can relate to. It is particularly important for more junior women to see and feel that they have senior leadership potential.
- The impact that assumptions can have on ambitions—and how being presumed to be the "tea-girl," notetaker, or assistant to a more junior male colleague, can be corrosive, demoralizing, and undermining of confidence. Assumptions of inferiority can have a devastating impact on women's careers.
- Additional barriers for women of color and women who have disabilities. Perhaps most significantly, intersectionality lands a heavy blow for women with more than one protected characteristic. Time and again, women told us about the many additional barriers they face. Unless women from diverse backgrounds are promoted to the top tier, it signals that they are not wanted there, and, as one participant told us, "There is a push for women at the top but there isn't really any push for ethnic minorities . . . as you go higher and higher the color seems to fade."[4]

Male Champions for Change

We also held many "Male Champions for Change" roundtables to bring together senior male leaders in law to discuss ways to improve equality and diversity in the legal profession. Although a smaller series than the domestic or international roundtables, the findings were no less insightful.

The men acknowledged that women are significantly underrepresented in senior positions in the legal services sector. It was felt that this imbalance, in turn, has led to a larger gender pay gap, mainly, but not exclusively, due to the small percentage of women in senior positions.

As with the women's roundtables, the men identified the need to focus on female promotion. Looking further down the talent pipeline to ensure that women are gaining suitable experience and credibility in the early years and to ensure effective succession planning, senior leadership needs to play a more proactive part. As one participant put it, "If businesses don't change, women will vote with their feet."

4. *Id.* at 7–10.

Advocating for Change

We were incredibly fortunate throughout this program to work extensively with our international colleagues. Globally, we held 35 roundtables in 21 cities across 18 jurisdictions involving more than 700 lawyers. The ABA International Law Section and the ABA Commission on Women in the Profession hosted roundtables.

Our *International Women in Law Report: Advocating for Change* produced some surprising findings.[5] We anticipated that the experiences of women across the world would vary significantly, but, although some of the accounts were quite frankly eye-watering, our findings evidenced that the challenges and experiences of female lawyers are remarkably similar across the globe.

There are shared experiences in relation to traditional gender roles and stereotypes, particularly gender pay disparity and the lack of flexible working.

Around the world, there are social and cultural expectations about how women should behave because of their gender. This was especially felt by working mothers who are penalized for their additional caregiving commitments outside of work.

There is also a serious lack of transparency about financial compensation across all regions. This prevents the identification of pay discrepancies and undermines or prevents accountability for ensuring fair remuneration and equal treatment.

Solutions

In spite of the barriers to progression, there is hope.

From the survey, we identified some solutions:

- Ensuring access to and mainstreaming of flexible working for all;
- Providing mentoring and sponsorship;
- Having visible role models for gender equality—men as well as women; and

---

5. *See* Law Society of England & Wales, International Women in Law Report: Advocating for Change: Transforming the Future of the Legal Profession Through Greater Gender Equality (2019), https://www.law.ox.ac.uk/sites/files/oxlaw/advocating_for_change_-_international_women_in_law_report.pdf.

- Crucially, engaging men in the debate. We need male leaders to be responsible for bringing about gender equality in their firms and businesses.

Among the three reports, we identified some further key solutions, including:

- Leading from the top and by example, ensuring business leaders walk the talk and demonstrate their active support for and engagement with strategies that develop inclusive workplaces;
- Placing diversity at the center of business planning and recognizing it as a priority in the same way as operational risk, compliance, and financial monitoring;
- Encouraging greater transparency, ranging from implementing clear policies on flexible working to reporting on business-wide statistics relating to gender and ethnicity pay;
- Providing consistent and reoccurring implicit bias training for all staff at all levels to make people aware of their biases and ensure they are not acting on them when making decisions about others;
- Assessing recruitment, selection, promotion, and remuneration policies so that objective decisions are made based on competencies, quality, and attributes;
- Having bystander training to support others to "call it out," implementing gender champions, and having gender balance on any decision-making body; and
- Making flexible working available to everyone at all levels of seniority by focusing on contributions made rather than time spent in the office.

In June 2019, we held an international symposium, which was attended by hundreds of lawyers from across the globe. At this conference, we launched the "Women in Law Pledge," an initiative led by all the representative bodies in the United Kingdom and leading firms and legal businesses from across the profession, and supported by the UK government.[6]

Signatories to the pledge commit to work together to address gender inequality. This includes tackling discrimination, bullying, and harassment in the workplace; challenging the gender pay gap in our organizations; appointing a senior and accountable champion; addressing

6. Press Release, Law Society of England & Wales, Women in Law Pledge, June 16, 2020, https://www.lawsociety.org.uk/campaigns/women-in-leadership-in-law/tools/the-women-in-law-pledge.

discriminatory workplace cultures and bias; and publishing targets and action plans. It's all about accountability, and it has international application.

Imagine the change if every law firm and legal business not only signed up but also implemented and enforced this pledge. It would be truly transformational.

As a profession that strives to uphold justice, we must be at the forefront of the fight for gender equality and diversity in the workplace.

The work that we undertook at the Law Society of England and Wales arms us with the information about the barriers that are faced by women and sets out the actions that can and must be taken by men and women. There is no acceptable excuse to not act.

It is beholden upon all of us to be activists to make sure that, globally, our profession is one we can be proud of, that clearly reflects how it embraces diversity and inclusion, and that properly represents those whom it services. We need a cultural shift in the legal sector, and, for that, we all need to be part of the solution.

Each one of us can and must make a positive difference.

10

United States: Our Sheroes Have Always Been Clan Mothers: What America Learned about Suffrage from Native Women

The Honorable Lisa Atkinson[1]

We hold these truths to be self-evident, that all men are created equal, that they are endowed by their Creator with certain unalienable Rights, that among these are Life, Liberty and the pursuit of Happiness.

—Preamble to the Declaration of Independence, 1776

This shining and inspirational language contained within the Declaration of Independence is taught in school as proof that we have formed "the" most perfect type of government in all of the world. As originally drafted and understood, however, these words were intended to apply to White and largely Protestant male landowners from England. They were mainly not intended to apply to the Irish, Italians, Catholics, Jews, and enslaved Africans who had been kidnapped and brought here as slaves (many of whom were owned by the drafters of the Declaration), or to the "merciless Indian Savages"[2] who inhabited this continent for thousands of years

1. Judge Lisa L. Atkinson has been a tribal court hearing officer/trial judge/appellate justice for over 20 years, having served over 40 tribes throughout the United States. Judge Atkinson currently resides in the beautiful state of Hawaii. This chapter was written and submitted in early 2020; any publishing delays were not within the author's control. The opinions shared in this essay are those of the author and are not claimed to represent any particular Native American Indian Nation.

2. A mere 30 lines below "all men are created equal," the Declaration of Independence cites as justification for throwing off British rule that the King ". . . has excited domestic insurrections amongst us, and has endeavoured [sic] to bring on

prior to the British occupations. And these words most certainly were not to be applied to women, much less Indian (Native)[3] women.

Ironically, the most important document in our country's history, the U.S. Constitution, was fashioned after the Great Law of Peace,[4] established by these same "merciless Indian Savages," the Iroquois Confederacy,[5] more than three centuries earlier.[6] Even more ironically, a key to the Iroquois Confederacy's successful democracy was the role of women in positions of power and decision-making.

What does this have to do with the 19th Amendment to the U.S. Constitution and to Native women in particular? It shows a pattern of how Native ideas and practices have been co-opted by White people and thereby deemed worthy or acceptable. The 19th Amendment is but one more example.

The Suffragists and Influence from Indian Country

The women's suffragist movement began around 1848 and lasted until the 19th Amendment was adopted in 1920. It took more than 70 years from the origins of the movement for women to secure the right to vote. As elementary children, we all learned about the suffragists and how women "won" the right to vote in our country. In my case, we even put

---

the inhabitants of our frontiers, ***the merciless Indian Savages, whose known rule of warfare, is an undistinguished destruction of all ages, sexes and conditions***" (bold emphasis added).

3. The terms "Indian" and "Native" will be used interchangeably in this chapter. This author prefers "Native"; however, under the laws of the United States, the term is "Indian."

4. Also known as the "Iroquois Confederacy and Great Law of Peace" or the "Iroquois Constitution." Historians, both tribal and nontribal, have not conclusively established the date that the Iroquois Great Law of Peace was established. Estimates are that it was made between 1100 and 1450. It was an oral law, passed down from generation to generation, and said to have taken eight to nine days to say. It was transcribed into written English by Seth Newhouse, a Mohawk, in 1880.

5. The Iroquois Confederacy, also known as the Haudenosaunee Confederacy, was comprised of five formerly warring tribes—Mohawk, Oneida, Cayuga, Seneca, and Onondaga (later joined by the Tuscarora)—who created a peaceful alliance through the adoption of the principles contained in the Great Law of Peace.

6. *See* H.R. Con. Res. 331, 100th Cong. (1988) (a Concurrent Resolution to acknowledge the contribution of the Iroquois Confederacy of Nations to the development of the U.S. Constitution).

on a school play about it.[7] But we did not learn the backstory on where the leaders of the movement found inspiration and support for their fight. A number of the suffragists credited with securing the 19th Amendment's passage lived in and around Iroquois territory in New York state and had occasion to meet and learn about women's roles in the Iroquois Confederacy.

Lucretia Coffin Mott

In 1848, Lucretia Coffin Mott and her husband spent the summer among the Seneca Indians, one of the tribes in the Iroquois Confederacy, where she observed the leadership roles that women held in the tribe, including the responsibilities of selecting and removing chiefs and the power to veto any act of war.[8]

> Lucretia Mott saw this world in practice when she and her husband visited the Seneca in the summer of 1848. She watched women who had equal responsibilities with men in all aspects of their lives—family, spiritual, government, economic. At this time the Seneca women were deeply involved in the decision of whether or not to drop their traditional clan system of government and adopt the constitutional form insisted upon by the Quakers. While the Cattaraugus Seneca finally did accept the United States model, they refused to accept the element of male dominance. They placed in their constitution that no treaty would be valid without the approval of three-fourths of the "mothers of the nation."[9]

Later that summer, Mott rallied those gathered at the famous women's rights convention at Seneca Falls to fight for many of the rights she had witnessed the Iroquois women exercising, including the right to vote. The result of the Seneca Falls Convention was the creation and adoption of the Declaration of Sentiments, written by Elizabeth Cady Stanton, which mirrored much of the language of the Declaration of Independence, but

---

7. At best, the play was tangentially about the suffragists. Written in 1982 for school drama clubs and titled, "Billy Bart: Scourge of the West," it involved a man tying a woman to the railroad tracks as "tribal warriors" prepared to attack him. It was not what we would call "appropriate" in its depiction of Natives or Wild West villains, yet alone suffragists.

8. *See* Sally Roesch Wagner, *Iroquois Women Inspire 19th Century Feminists*, NAT'L NOW TIMES (Summer 1999), http://www.peacecouncil.net/NOON/Haudwomen.htm.

9. *Id.*

with the perspective of men as the oppressors rather than the king of England.[10] Efforts to secure suffrage stalled, however, when the country became embroiled in the Civil War. After the war, the movement again gained steam and new warriors.

Matilda Josyln Gage

Elizabeth Cady Stanton's contemporary, Matilda Joslyn Gage, wrote in 1893 that:

> The famous Iroquois Indians, or Six Nations, . . . showed alike in form of government, and in social life, reminiscences of the Matriarchate. The line of descent, feminine, was especially notable in all tribal relations such as the election of Chiefs, and the Council of Matrons, to which all disputed questions were referred for final adjudication. No sale of lands was valid without consent of the squaws[11] and among the State Archives at Albany, New York, treaties are preserved signed by the "Sachems and Principal Women of the Six Nations." The women also possessed the veto power on questions of war. Sir William Johnston mentions an instance of Mohawk squaws forbidding the war-path to young braves. The family relation among the Iroquois demonstrated woman's superiority in power. When an Indian husband brought the products of the chase to the wigwam, his control over it ceased. In the home, the wife was absolute; the sale of the skins was regulated by her, the price was paid to her. If for any cause the Iroquois husband and wife separated, the wife took with her all the property she had brought into the wigwam; the children also accompanied the mother, whose right to them was recognized as supreme. So fully to this day is descent reckoned through the mother, that blue-eyed, fair-haired children of white fathers are numbered in the tribe and receive both from state and nation their portion of the yearly dole paid to Indian tribes. . . . But the most notable fact connected with woman's participation

10. *See Declaration of Sentiments and Resolutions* in 1 Elizabeth Cady Stanton, Susan B. Anthony, and M.J. Cage. A History of Woman Suffrage (1889), https://www.womenshistory.org/resources/primary-source/declaration-sentiments-and-resolution; *Nat'l Historical Park N.Y. History: Declaration of Sentiments*, Nat'l Park Serv., https://www.nps.gov/wori/learn/historyculture/declaration-of-sentiments.htm (providing the list of signers) (last visited June 1, 2021).

11. *Squaw* is a highly offensive and disfavored term. It is included here to retain the integrity of the quotation as originally written.

> in governmental affairs among the Iroquois is the statement of Hon. George Bancroft that the form of government of the United States, was borrowed from that of the Six Nations. Thus to the Matriarchate or Mother-rule is the modern world indebted for its first conception of inherent rights, natural equality of condition, and the establishment of a civilized government upon this basis. Although the reputation of the Iroquois as warriors appears most prominent in history, we nevertheless find their real principles to have been the true Matriarchal one of peace and industry. . . . Their history was preserved by means of wampum, while under their women the science of government reached the highest form known to the world.[12]

Early Native Female Champions of Native Rights, Including the Right to Vote

Zitkala-Ša

Zitkala-Ša, a Yankton Sioux citizen (1876–1938) (boarding school name: Gertrude Simmons; married name: Gertrude Simmons Bonnin), was taken from her home on the Yankton Indian Reservation in South Dakota when she was eight years old and placed in an Indian boarding school in Indiana. Unsurprisingly, when she was able to leave the school and return home, she felt that she no longer belonged on her reservation, so she left again and attended Earlham College in Indiana and then the New England Conservatory of Music in Boston. She then went on to teach music at the Carlisle Industrial Indian School in Pennsylvania, which was founded by Captain Daniel Pratt of "kill the Indian in him, and save the man" notoriety.[13]

After seeing the harmful cultural, physical, and mental effects that boarding school life had on Indian students, Zitkala-Ša began writing articles criticizing the system.[14] Zitkala-Ša believed that Indigenous

12. Matilda Joslyn Gage, Woman, Church & State: The Original Exposé of Male Collaboration Against the Female Sex 9–10 (Project Gutenberg 2014) (1893), https://www.gutenberg.org/files/45580/45580-h/45580-h.htm.

13. *History Matters: "Kill the Indian, and Save the Man," Capt. Richard H. Pratt on the Education of Native Americans*, GMU, http://historymatters.gmu.edu/d/4929/ (excerpt of a paper read by Captain Daniel Pratt, the founder of Carlisle Industrial Indian School, at a 1892 conference) (last visited June 1, 2021).

14. Zitkala-Ša was a contributor to *Atlantic Monthly* and *Harper's Monthly*, among other publications.

people in America should be American citizens with the right to vote: "In the land that was once his own—America . . . there was never a time more opportune than now for America to enfranchise the Red man!"[15] She argued that Indians should be represented by the system of government imposed upon them as the original inhabitants of this country.[16]

In 1926, Zitkala-Ša and her husband General Raymond T. Bonnin (also of Yankton descent) founded the National Council of American Indians, which existed until Raymond's death in 1942. The purpose of the council was to "Help Indians help themselves in protecting their rights and priorities."[17] Zitkala-Ša served as president, fundraiser, and speaker of the council from its formation until her death. One of the goals of the council was to achieve suffrage for all Indians. The council was a precursor to the National Congress of American Indians, which continues to this day.[18]

Unsurprisingly, I had never heard of Zitkala-Ša until I began researching this piece. In the history of women's suffrage, most of the attention is paid to the White women who are credited with getting the 19th Amendment adopted. Women of color, including Zitkala-Ša, are rarely mentioned, and, if they are, it is often in a footnote. The work and the traditional governmental practices of matrilineal tribes and Native suffragists therefore are rarely, if ever, mentioned.

Marie Louise Bottineau Baldwin

Marie Louise Bottineau Baldwin (1863–1952), Turtle Mountain Band of Chippewa Indians of North Dakota, was an attorney who advocated for tribal rights and women's suffrage. Marie joined the Society of American Indians (SAI), where she worked alongside Zitkala-Ša on advancing the cause of Native women's suffrage. Marie traveled the country speaking on the issues and educating the public about traditional political roles of women in tribal societies. Marie also testified before Congress and was part of a group that met with then-president Woodrow Wilson in 1914 to discuss suffrage.[19] After working in her father's law firm and

---

15. Zitkala-Ša (as Gertrude Bonnin), *Editorial Comment*, 6 AM. INDIAN MAG. 192 (1919) (writing in her role as the editor of the magazine).

16. *Id.*

17. *See* Constitution and By-Laws of National Council of American Indians (1926), https://acdc.amherst.edu/view/asc:407646/asc:407685.

18. NATIONAL CONGRESS OF AMERICAN INDIANS, http:///ncai.org (last visited June 1, 2021).

19. *Marie Louise Bottineau Baldwin*, U.S. NAT'L PARK SERV., https://www.nps.gov/people/marie-louise-bottineau-baldwin.htm (last visited June 1, 2021).

being appointed as a clerk in the Office of Indian Affairs, a precursor to the Bureau of Indian Affairs, by President Theodore Roosevelt, Baldwin attended and completed law school in 1914 at the age of 51, becoming the first Native woman and first woman of color to graduate from the Washington College of Law.[20] While in law school, she marched with lawyers in the 1913 Suffrage Parade, organized by Alice Paul.[21] She remained politically active in support of the 19th Amendment and then the passage of the Indian Citizenship Act four years later in 1924, which expanded suffrage to more Native women.[22]

How many young Native girls know the history of Zitkala-Ša and Marie Louise Bottineau Baldwin? I know I did not. My education would have been richer and felt more inclusive if I had known that my foremothers had played a prominent role in securing my right to vote.

Federal Legislation and Litigation

Indian Citizenship Act of 1924

Four years after the passage of the 19th Amendment guaranteeing women's right to vote, the United States passed the Indian Citizenship Act of 1924, also known as the Snyder Act.[23] Until that time, Indians were not deemed "citizens" of the United States and, therefore, did not enjoy the rights guaranteed by the U.S. Constitution. The original inhabitants of this country, my ancestors, were not considered citizens, despite having served (and continuing to serve) in the military disproportionately to our numbers and in every single military action this country has fought. Prior to the passage of the Indian Citizenship Act, the only way an Indian could become a citizen, subject to consent by a state or the U.S. government, was to renounce his/her tribal citizenship, serve in the military, accept a

20. *See* Hilary Parkinson, *19th Amendment at 100: Mary Louise Bottineau Baldwin*, U.S. NAT'L ARCHIVES (Apr. 2, 2020), https://prologue.blogs.archives.gov/2020/04/02/19th-amendment-at-100-mary-louise-bottineau-baldwin/.

21. *Id.*

22. *See Counting Down to the 100th Anniversary of the 19th Amendment with #19SuffrageStories*, U.S. NAT'L ARCHIVES (Aug. 3, 2020), https://prologue.blogs.archives.gov/2020/08/03/counting-down-to-the-100th-anniversary-of-the-19th-amendment-with-19suffragestories/.

23. Indian Citizenship Act of 1924, Pub. L. No. 68–175, ch. 233, 43 Stat. 253 (1924) (codified as amended at 8 U.S.C. § 1401(b)).

land allotment, marry a White person, pay taxes, and/or live among the Whites as one of them.[24]

It would seem to be understood that upon the passage of the Indian Citizenship Act, all Indians would now enjoy the full benefits and protections guaranteed by the U.S. Constitution, including but not limited to the right to vote. But that was not the case.

Litigating for the Native Right to Vote

The Indian Citizenship Act, while confirming Indian citizenship, did nothing to secure the rights of Native people to vote. The authority to determine voting rights was reserved to the individual states under the U.S. Constitution. Most of the states did not allow Natives to vote, so litigation challenging restrictive state voting laws, constitutional clauses, and judicial decisions became the vehicle to secure and/or confirm Native suffrage.[25]

In 1948, more than 20 years after Native citizenship was conveyed, the Arizona Supreme Court issued its decision in *Harrison v. Laveen*, confirming the voting rights of Indians in Arizona.[26] In New Mexico that same year, in an unreported case entitled *Trujillo v. Garley*, a panel of three judges held that a Pueblo Indian did have the right to vote in U.S. elections.[27] The different statuses of Indians within New Mexico (pueblo Indians versus treaty Indians) and their ability to vote was not

---

24. *See, e.g.*, Act of November 6, 1919, ch. 95, 41 Stat. 350 (1919) (granting citizenship to certain Indians who served in World War I); Elk v. Wilkins, 112 U.S. 94 (1884) (finding that an Indian man, John Elk, who had voluntarily renounced his tribal citizenship but who had not been naturalized or taxed, was not a citizen under the 14th Amendment); Dred Scott v. Sandford, 60 U.S. 383 at 404 (1856) (denying Dred Scott, an African American man, the rights of citizenship and contrasting with the process of citizenship for Indians by legislation and treaty).

25. *See* Daniel McCool et al., Native Vote: American Indians, the Voting Rights Act, and the Right to Vote 9–10 (2007); *cf. Classroom Materials: Voting Rights for Native Americans*, Library of Congress, https://www.loc.gov/classroom-materials/elections/right-to-vote/voting-rights-for-native-americans/ (quoting a resident of Maine in 1930, "[T]he Indians aren't allowed to have a voice in state affairs because they aren't voters. . . . Just why the Indians shouldn't vote is something I can't understand. One of the Indians went over to Old Town once to see some official in the city hall about voting. I don't know just what position that official had over there, but he said to the Indian, 'We don't want you people over here. You have your own elections over on the island, and if you want to vote, go over there.'") (last visited June 1, 2021).

26. *See* Harrison v. Laveen, 196 P.2d 456 (Ariz. 1948).

27. *See* Trujillo v. Garley, Civ. No. 1353 (D.N.M. 1948).

clarified until *Montoya v. Bolack* was decided in 1962 by the New Mexico Supreme Court.[28] In *Montoya*, the court held:

> We are convinced that, for voting purposes, there is nothing in our constitution or in the statutes which prohibits an Indian from voting in a proper election, provided he fulfills the statutory requirements required of any other voter. This being true, there can be no question but that the reservation is a part of the state, and residence for voting purposes, within the meaning of art. VII, § 1, N.M.Const., follows.[29]

Voting Rights Act of 1965

The Voting Rights Act of 1965 was passed to prohibit states and local governments from any kind of measure that would "deny or abridge the right of any citizen of the United States to vote on account of race or color."[30] Through this act, the federal government assumed enforcement authority over states and localities to uphold the act. Several states were put under strict federal supervision, called "preclearance," to monitor their compliance. In 2013, the U.S. Supreme Court addressed two sections of the Voting Rights Act related to preclearance through its decision in *Shelby County v. Holder*.[31] In *Shelby*, the Court ruled that section 4(b) of the act containing the formula used for determining which state and local jurisdictions required preclearance under section 5 was unconstitutional given more contemporary data since the act's passage in 1965.[32] The Court did not address the constitutionality of the preclearance requirement under section 5.

Among those put under federal supervision prior to *Shelby County* were several states with high populations of Native Americans, including Alabama (one federally recognized tribe), Alaska (231 federally recognized tribes/villages), Arizona (21 federally recognized tribes), Louisiana (four federally recognized tribes), Mississippi (one federally recognized tribe), South Carolina (one federally recognized tribe), Virginia (seven federally recognized tribes), and a number of counties within other states, including the following:

---

28. *See* Montoya v. Bolack, 372 P.2d 387 (N.M. 1962).

29. *Id.* at 394.

30. Voting Rights Act of 1965, Pub. L. No. 89-110, 79 Stat. 437 (1965) (codified as amended in scattered sections of 42 and 52 U.S.C.); 52 U.S.C. § 10301.

31. *See* Shelby Cnty. v. Holder, 570 U.S. 529 (2013).

32. *Id.*

- California—Kings County (home of the Santa Rosa Indian Community of the Santa Rosa Rancheria) and Yuba County (Enterprise Rancheria of Maidu Indians)
- South Dakota—Oglala Lakota (home of the Pine Ridge Indian Reservation) and Todd Counties (home of the Rosebud Indian Reservation)
- North Carolina—Jackson County North Carolina (home of the Eastern Band of Cherokee Indians)[33]

All 50 states now guarantee, on paper, the right to vote to the Native citizens within their borders. In practice, however, there are still many obstacles—intentional or otherwise—that keep Native people from exercising this right. The population of American Indians and Alaska Natives in the United States is approximately 6.9 million.[34] Thirty-four percent of eligible Native voters are not registered to vote, according to the Native Vote project, a nonpartisan campaign initiated by the National Congress of American Indians.[35] That is 1.2 million unregistered eligible voters.[36] Native voters continue to face numerous challenges to voting, in addition to intimidation and threats. Some of those challenges, among many others, are:

- Extreme distances to voting locations, sometimes more than 300 miles roundtrip;
- Transportation issues (even for urban Indians, the polling place may be on the other side of the city);
- Address issues (many reservation homes do not have street addresses, with mail sent to "General Delivery" because in small and remote communities there may only be a centralized post office with P.O. boxes available and no home delivery);
- Homelessness or couch-surfing;

33. *Jurisdictions Previously Covered by Section 5*, U.S. Dep't of Justice, https://www.justice.gov/crt/jurisdictions-previously-covered-section-5 (last visited June 1, 2021, last updated Sept. 11, 2020); *cf. Tribal Leaders Directory*, U.S. Dep't of the Interior Indian Affairs, https://www.bia.gov/service/tribal-leaders-directory (searchable directory and map) (last visited July 20, 2022).

34. *Facts for Features: American Indian and Alaska Native Heritage Month: November 2020*, U.S. Census Bureau (Sept. 30, 2020), https://www.census.gov/newsroom/facts-for-features/2020/aian-month.html.

35. *Native Vote Infographic*, Native Vote (May 2020), http://www.nativevote.org/wp-content/uploads/2020/05/2020-Native-Vote-Infographic.pdf.

36. *Id.*

- Identification challenges (not everyone has a valid state-issued driver's license or ID card; not everyone has a birth certificate; some Native people were renamed at boarding schools, and those names do not match birth certificates); and
- Language barriers for older tribal members who primarily speak their Native languages (particularly in rural Alaska and within the Navajo Nation).

Clearly, for Native people, the *right* to vote does not mean the *ability* to vote, at least not without overcoming significant obstacles, which can lead to disenfranchising those 1.2 million eligible but unregistered tribal voters.

Why Native Women Voting Matters

Although women gained the right to vote in 1920 and Indians became citizens in 1924, Natives and Native women still faced (and continue to face) many obstacles in exercising their ability to vote. States overwhelmingly passed laws and policies continuing to prohibit or make it nearly impossible for Native people to vote (regardless of sex). There have been poll taxes,[37] literacy tests,[38] language tests,[39] identification requirements,[40] address requirements,[41] and voting location challenges,[42] intermixed with

37. *See, e.g.*, Harper v. Virginia Bd. of Elections, 383 U.S. 663 (1966) (holding that poll taxes violated the Equal Protection Clause of the 14th Amendment and discriminated against the poor). The attempt to correct the poll tax nationwide was through the passage of the 24th Amendment in 1964, as ratified by two-thirds of the states, 44 years after the 19th Amendment was passed and 40 years after the Indian Citizenship Act.

38. *See, e.g.*, Oregon v. Mitchell, 400 U.S. 112 (1970) (upholding the ban on literacy tests under the 1970 Amendments to the Voting Rights Act and discussing the 14th, 15th, 19th, and 24th Amendments to the U.S. Constitution).

39. *Id.* at 129; Katzenback v. Morgan, 384 U.S. 641 (1966).

40. The recent voter ID case out of North Dakota, *Brakebill v. Jaeger*, 932 F.3d 671 (2019), illustrates the continued struggle Reservation residents face in exercising their rights to vote. In this case, which has since been resolved through a consent decree, Parties agreed that on-Reservation voters may use tribal IDs and tribally designated street addresses for proof of residency and eligibility.

41. *Id.*

42. *See, e.g.*, Brnovich, Att'y Gen. of Az. v. Democratic Nat'l Comm., Nos. 19-1257, 19-1258 (U.S. cert. granted Oct. 2, 2020; arguments scheduled Mar. 2, 2021) (consolidating with Arizona Republican Party v. Democratic Nat'l Comm. to consider whether an Arizona law that makes it a felony to collect and turn in the ballot of another, even with that person's permission, violates the Voting Rights Act or the 15th Amendment), *appealing* 948 F.3d 989 (9th Cir. 2020) (en banc) (finding the law illegal).

intimidation, violence, and threats of violence for those who would dare exercise their right to vote.

Why would anyone seek to deny the Native right to vote? Because voting means power. Power to elect legislators who look, think, and act in ways that are in line with Native beliefs, goals, and values. Power to influence legislative bodies to enact legislation to further Native interests, protect Native people, and protect Native resources. Power to repeal past legislation that had disproportionate effects on the lives of Native and other marginalized populations. And because Native voters, like many from marginalized communities, tend to vote overwhelmingly for more inclusive candidates and policies. Following are just two examples of why Native votes, and Native women's votes, are crucial to cultural survival.

Policies of Sterilizing Native Women in the 1970s

In the 1970s, the federal government, through doctors working for and with the Indian Health Service, engaged in a practice against Native women that would shock the conscience of many, if they'd known at the time that it was happening. They sterilized thousands of Native women without their knowledge and/or proper consent.[43] *Read that again. They sterilized thousands of Native women without their knowledge and/or proper consent.* While this seems horrific generally, the practice targeted "full-blooded Indian women for sterilization procedures."[44] In 1976, the U.S. General Accounting Office (GAO) acknowledged the practice and estimated that the procedure at *just* "4 of the 12 Indian Health Service regions sterilized 3,406 American Indian women without their permission between 1973 and 1976. The GAO [found] that 36 women under age 21 were sterilized during this period despite a court-ordered moratorium on sterilizations of women younger than 21."[45] These crimes[46] occurred at government-operated facilities, as well as at private and secular facilities.

---

43. *1976: Government Admits Unauthorized Sterilization of Women*, U.S. NAT'L LIBRARY OF MEDICINE, https://www.nlm.nih.gov/nativevoices/timeline/543.html (last visited June 1, 2021).

44. *Id.* (citing an independent study by Dr. Connie Pinkerton-Uni (Choctaw/Cherokee), whose research discovered that one in four American Indian women had been sterilized without her consent).

45. *Id.*; U.S. GOV'T ACCOUNTABILITY OFFICE, PUB. NO. HRD-77-3, INVESTIGATION OF ALLEGATIONS CONCERNING INDIAN HEALTH SERVICE 4 (1976), https://www.gao.gov/products/HRD-77-3.

46. I use the term "crimes" as these procedures would have been considered assault under the ruling in *Schoendorff v. Society of New York Hosp.*, 105 N.E. 92 (N.Y. 1914), wherein Justice Benjamin Cardoza stated that "every human being of adult years and sound mind has a right to determine what shall be done with his own

The total estimates of Native women who were involuntarily sterilized during this time is likely at least 25 percent of all those of child-bearing age—an estimated 70,000 women.[47]

How do you kill culture? You remove its children. Or in this case, you remove the ability for there to be children to whom cultural knowledge is transmitted. As Cheyenne tribal judge Marie Sanchez stated, "the Native American woman is the carrier of our nation."[48] A number of Native advocates, including physicians, politicians, and reproductive rights supporters, fought to bring to light the crimes committed against Native women who were involuntarily sterilized.[49] How was this practice ended? Litigation. Court battles resulted in mandates for new patient consent procedures,[50] and, thus, laws and new regulations being adopted requiring true informed consent prior to sterilization.[51] Laws that were drafted and adopted by politicians who were put into office by voters.

VAWA, MMIW, and Voting for Legislators Who Will Pass Laws and Do Something

In more recent years, awareness about the staggering numbers of domestic violence victims and Missing and Murdered Indigenous Women (MMIW), Girls, and Two Spirit persons has been gaining attention beyond our tribal communities. While these crises have been recognized for decades within our U.S. and Canadian Native communities, national and international attention has been slow to understand the magnitude of the problem.

---

body; and a surgeon who performs an operation without his patient's consent commits an assault." *Id.* at 93.

47. Jane Lawrence, *The Indian Health Service and the Sterilization of Native American Women*, 24 Am. Indian Q. 400, 400 (2000), https://www.jstor.org/stable/1185911.

48. *Id.* at 412.

49. *See, e.g.*, Sally J. Torpy, *Native American Women and Coerced Sterilization: On the Trail of Tears in the 1970's*, 24 Am. Indian Culture & Res. J. (2000), https://www.law.berkeley.edu/php-programs/centers/crrj/zotero/loadfile.php?entity_key=QFDB5MW3.

50. *See, e.g.*, Relf v. Weinberger, 372 F. Supp. 1196 (D.C. Cir. 1974) (declaring the Sterilization Restrictions regulations used by federally funded health clinics to be "arbitrary and unreasonable" due to the lack of informed patient consent requirements and ordering, in part, the defendants to "promptly amend" the Sterilization Restrictions regulations).

51. *See, e.g.*, 42 C.F.R. §§ 441.253–.258 (2010) (requiring disclosures to the patient and a patient's informed consent for sterilization procedures).

Native women are subjected to violence at staggering rates, including murder rates more than ten times the national average.[52] In a 2010 study from the U.S. Department of Justice's National Institute of Justice, the author found that more than four in five American Indian and Alaska Native women (84.3 percent) have experienced violence in their lifetime, including:

- 56.1 percent who have experienced sexual violence;
- 55.5 percent who have experienced physical violence by an intimate partner;
- 48.8 percent who have experienced stalking; and
- 66.4 percent who have experienced psychological aggression by an intimate partner.[53]

"Overall, more than 1.5 million American Indian and Alaska Native women have experienced violence in their lifetime," according to the study.[54]

Of particular concern is the rate at which Native women are subjected to violence by non-Native perpetrators. Native female victims are 2.8 times as likely to have experienced violence by an interracial perpetrator as non-Hispanic White-only female victims (97 percent versus 35 percent); however, they are only 0.4 times as likely to have experienced violence by an intraracial (i.e., Native) perpetrator as non-Hispanic White-only female victims (35 percent versus 95 percent).[55]

Jurisdictional challenges often make reporting, finding, and prosecuting violence against Native women extremely difficult, which is where elected officials and critical litigation come into play. The 2013 reauthorization of the Violence Against Women Act[56] and the passage of the Tribal Law and Order Act[57] finally provided some *actual* results in the fight for protection of Native victims of violence. Within these pieces of legislation are provisions authorizing tribes to once again prosecute non-Indian perpetrators who commit violence against Indians on Indian

---

52. *See* Andre B. Rosay, PhD, Nat'l Inst. of Justice, U.S. Dep't of Justice, Research Report on Violence Against American Indian and Alaska Native Women and Men 1 (2016), https://www.ncjrs.gov/pdffiles1/nij/249736.pdf.

53. *Id.* at 2, 44.

54. *Id.* at 44.

55. *Id.* at 46.

56. Violence Against Women Reauthorization Act of 2013 (VAWA 2013), Pub. L. No. 113-4, 42 U.S.C. §§ 13701–14040.

57. Tribal Law and Order Act of 2010 (TLOA), Pub. L. No. 111-211, (codified as amended in scattered sections of 18 and 25 U.S.C.).

reservations.[58] The Tribal Law and Order Act created within it the authorization to appoint Special Assistant U.S. Attorneys (SAUSAs) and provided for enhanced tribal sentencing provisions to give tribal courts the ability to prosecute and sentence non-Indian perpetrators who are found guilty of the crimes enumerated within the act.[59] The inclusion of these "controversial" provisions was hard-fought in the halls of Congress and took the work of so many Native voters and allies around the country.

The Power of Native Women's Votes and Legislative Representation

In 2020, two bipartisan bills to combat the MMIW crisis became law: Savanna's Act[60] and the Not Invisible Act.[61] They aim to increase coordination, data collection, and transparency between tribes and law enforcement agencies. Savana's Act was named for a 22-year-old Spirit Lake tribal member in North Dakota who was murdered and had her eight-month-old fetus cut from her womb in 2017. The bill was introduced in 2017 by Senator Heidi Heitkamp, the first woman elected to the U.S. Senate from North Dakota, and was reintroduced in 2019 by Senator Lisa Murkowski from Alaska, a state with disproportionately high rates of MMIW,[62] with co-sponsorship by Senator Tom Udall from New Mexico. The Not Invisible Act of 2019 was sponsored by Senator Catherine Cortez Masto from Nevada, Senator Murkowski, and Senator John Tester from Montana, and co-sponsored by Senator Udall. The two bills were introduced in the House of Representatives by four members of federally

58. Tribes had exercised this right until the U.S. Supreme Court wrongly decided the case of *Oliphant v. Suquamish Indian Tribe*, 435 U.S. 191 (1978), which stripped tribes of the ability to prosecute crimes committed by non-Indians on Indian Reservations.

59. Prior to the passage of TLOA, tribes were limited in sentencing any offender to no more than one year incarceration and no more than a $5,000 fine per offense, pursuant to the language contained in the Indian Civil Rights Act of 1968. 25 U.S.C. §§ 1301–1304 (1968). For tribes authorized to prosecute and sentence under TLOA, penalties may now be up to three years' incarceration and up to $15,000 per offense under § 1302(b).

60. Savanna's Act, Pub. L. No. 116-165 (2020).

61. Not Invisible Act, Pub. L. No. 116-166 (2020).

62. *Alaska*, Nat'l Indian Country Clearinghouse on Sexual Assault, https://www.niccsa.org/alaska/ (Alaska Natives comprise less than 20 percent of the state's population, yet Native women comprise 54 percent of the reported sexual assaults) (last visited June 1, 2021).

recognized tribes: Deb Haaland (Pueblo of Laguna), Tom Cole (Chickasaw Nation), Sharice Davids (Ho-Chunk Nation), and Markwayne Mullin (Cherokee Nation). In 2020, voters returned the four to Congress and also elected Yvette Herrell (Cherokee Nation) from New Mexico to serve in the 117th Congress beginning January 3, 2021, and ending January 3, 2023. In March 2021, Representative Haaland resigned from Congress upon her confirmation to become U.S. Secretary of the Interior, making history as the first Native American to lead a federal agency and to serve as a presidential cabinet member.

Notably, Senator Murkowski, a Republican from Alaska, won her Senate seat in 2010 as only one other Senator in the history of the U.S. Senate has—as a write-in candidate. The senator gave credit to her victory in the 2010 election to the significant power of the Alaska Native vote.[63] Senator Murkowski is not the only member of the U.S. Congress who owes her seat to the Native vote.[64] Senator John Tester won his 2018 reelection with the support of tribal communities within his state, as did Senator Maria Cantwell, who was formally endorsed by 12 tribes in the state of Washington. Senator Heidi Heitkamp from North Dakota won her 2012 election with a 1 percent margin that she credited to Native voters. Senator Tim Johnson's win in 2002 in South Dakota came from the final 500 votes being counted from the Pine Ridge Indian Reservation.

These actions demonstrate that the Native vote does matter, and legislative representation does have an impact.

Final Thoughts

The road to suffrage for Natives, and Native women, has been long and fraught with obstacles. The issues that affect our communities are no different than those that affect other communities, albeit often on an enhanced scale proportionate to our numbers. The historical and legal relationship between Indian Tribes and the United States has provided many challenges that have resulted in our disenfranchisement and marginalization. We continue to fight, however, to ensure that our people

63. *See* Becky Bohrer, *Murkowski Calls Write-In Victory 'Our Miracle,'* The Seattle Times (Nov. 18, 2010, 1:19 AM, updated 3:31 AM), https://www.seattletimes.com/seattle-news/politics/murkowski-calls-write-in-victory-our-miracle-1/.

64. *See, e.g.*, *Native Vote Infographic*, Native Vote (May 2020), http://www.nativevote.org/wp-content/uploads/2020/05/2020-Native-Vote-Infographic.pdf (describing the influence of the Native vote in electing Senators Marla Cantwell, Heidi Heitkamp, Tim Johnson, Lisa Murkowski, and John Tester).

are able to exercise all of their Inalienable Rights, including the precious right to vote. A new day is coming, and there is hope for a better future for our tribal communities through increased representation at every level of government. Hopefully, the next seven generations will know the names and stories of Zitkala-Ša,[65] Wilma Mankiller,[66] Diane Humetewa,[67] Sharice Davids, and Deb Haaland,[68] as well as many more Native women trailblazers who have made, and will continue to make, the world better for our people.

65. Women's suffrage advocate and founder of the National Council of American Indians (1926).

66. First woman elected Principal Chief of the Cherokee Nation of Oklahoma (1985).

67. First Native woman (Hopi) appointed to the federal judiciary (2014).

68. First two Native women elected to the U.S. Congress (2018), and Deb Haaland appointed as the U.S. Secretary of the Interior, becoming the first Native American to serve in the presidential cabinet (2021).

11

United States: Unresolved Accomplishments and Trailblazing Sheroes

Paulette Brown[1]

Fifty years ago as a spirited teen in the midst of the civil rights movement, I had no way of knowing what the future had in store for me as I thought about what I wanted to be and what I might achieve in this world. I grew up in segregated Baltimore in a country where racial, social, and economic disparities were often stark and unambiguous and where prosperity and opportunity remained stubbornly out of reach for millions of Black/African Americans, Native Americans, and other people of color. Although I personally was buffered from the riots and the violence at the time, the devastating effects of injustice, discrimination, and prejudice vexed me. How could my country serve as the world's melting pot and beacon of hope for its freedoms, democracy, and the great American Dream, yet still be so perplexingly incomplete in its delivery of justice, equality, access to opportunity, and multicultural inclusiveness?

My parents taught me, and the civil rights movement demonstrated, that the core essentials of our democracy—the constitutional, legal, and justice frameworks—provide us, the people, with the power to make our country better. As I looked to my future, I wanted to be an agent of change and to use every opportunity to make a positive difference.

1. Paulette Brown is founder and principal of MindSetPower, LLC, and a former partner and Chief Diversity and Inclusion Officer of an Am Law 100 firm. She was the first woman of color to lead the American Bar Association as its president (2015–2016) and a former president of the National Bar Association, the largest organization of predominantly African American lawyers and judges in the United States.

Trailblazing

My parents demonstrated time and time again that you cannot be afraid to speak up for what's right and fair. I similarly wanted to speak my mind and say the truth. And, I wanted a seat at the decision-making table, with all kinds of people at that table with me. I long learned from my family and in my career that, if you want to make a difference, to make somebody's life better, and to make a group of lives better, you need a lot of people—all kinds of people—at your table. Further, I needed to take people as they came to me; no one is no better than or less than anyone else.

My first vote was marvelously thrilling, yet, at the same, insufficient. The hard-won individual achievements of the Civil Rights Act of 1964,[2] the end of poll taxes with the ratification of the 24th Amendment in 1964,[3] and the Voting Rights Act of 1965 finally prohibiting racial discrimination in voting,[4] galvanized record-breaking numbers of Black/African American voters in the late 1960s.[5] Until 1965, restrictive state and local election laws and practices, as well as intimidation and violence, had been used as legal and extralegal tactics to disenfranchise and deny Black/African Americans and other people of color of their voting rights.[6] The expanded voter registration and voter turnout in those days had pushed the doors of democracy further open. Still, like many others, I dreamed of a day when those doors would be fully opened with all their rights for all. Full political participation would require eliminating the vestiges of those long-standing barriers and energizing Black/African Americans to continue to vote, become candidates, participate in political parties, and serve in positions in government at all levels, from the local mayor to the White House. Thus, there I was, ballot in hand, casting a vote that not only counted but also mattered.

---

2. Civil Rights Act of 1964, Pub. L. No. 88-353, 78 Stat. 241 (1964).

3. U.S. Const. amend. XXIV.

4. Voting Rights Act of 1965, Pub. L. No. 89-110, 79 Stat. 437 (1965).

5. Sarah Pruitt, *When Did African Americans Actually Get the Right to Vote?*, History (Jan. 29, 2020) (updated Apr. 15, 2021), https://www.history.com/news/african-american-voting-right-15th-amendment.

6. *See, e.g.*, Determination of the Attorney General Pursuant to Section 4(b)(1) of the Voting Rights Act of 1965, U.S. Dep't of Justice, 30 Fed. Reg. 9,897 (Aug. 7, 1965) (officially publishing the list of 21 states with unlawful discriminatory voting practices); Determination of the Director of the Census Pursuant to Section 4(b)(2) of the Voting Rights Act of 1965 (Pub. L. No. 89-110), U.S. Dep't of Commerce, 30 Fed. Reg. 9,897 (Aug. 7, 1965) (publishing a list of states and counties with discriminatory voting practices and less than 50 percent voter turnout in the recent presidential election).

In keeping with the common phrase that "all politics is local," my first elected position was just that. During my junior year at Howard University, I was elected class president and found myself transfixed by how a group of students, through student government, could work with the administration of the university to make changes requested by students.

At Seton Hall University School of Law, the law riveted me with how it can empower. I put my keen eye on fighting injustice, discrimination, and prejudice in all its forms and pursuing truth, dignity, and equality—in practice and in the law. I remember the day when I passed the bar exam. Like any newly minted lawyer, I remember vividly the sensation—the feeling of achievement and that all things are possible.

Among my fondest memories, during the first democratic elections in South Africa, I literally put the pedal to the metal driving a stick shift car on the left side of the road to transport our group of international electoral observers during three days of elections. As the president of the National Bar Association (NBA), the oldest and largest national network of predominantly African American attorneys and judges in the United States,[7] I was leading our delegation of lawyers and judges. I was literally leading our group as the driver because no one else in our delegation knew how to drive a stick shift. As international election observers, we provided independent oversight to help ensure fair elections and adherence to international standards and norms. We were dispatched to the Transkei area where Nelson Mandela is originally from and stayed in a hotel where Winnie Mandela was also staying.

During the elections, people turned out in droves, creating an air of hopeful excitement but also tremendously long lines and ballot shortages. We visited polling places at schools, prisons, and hospitals, with eager voters even being rolled from their hospital rooms on gurneys to vote. At one polling place, upon seeing all those people anxiously waiting yet unable to vote because they didn't have enough ballots, my adrenaline vaulted me forward with pavement-pounding purpose and determination—no potential voter will be left behind on my watch! Running to a nearby polling place, I gathered up their extras and returned with ballots. Everybody got to vote. It was amazing and a distinct personal honor to be part of that unforgettable moment in history when Apartheid's legally institutionalized racial segregation ended and millions of voters from all

7. *See* National Bar Association, https://nationalbar.org (last visited June 19, 2021).

racial groups, roughly 87 percent of all eligible voters, took to the ballot box to determine their collective future.[8]

Lawyers are not accustomed to looking the other way when there are threats to democracy, justice, or the rule of law. Like many, I have spent a significant portion of my career advocating for equality under the law, individual rights, and changes in the profession and public institutions to help ensure the public's faith in the fairness of our laws and their trust in those who make, enforce, practice, and administer our laws.

As a lawyer, and as a woman lawyer of color, my career has been filled with many "firsts" and trailblazing moments of achievement. Among them, I have had the satisfaction of creating new trails for women's participation in the law and in leadership positions within the legal field and society. Throughout my life, I have always been curious to know who has been left out, who has not received credit, and who has not been included. Matters of diversity and inclusion run through my veins. If I would accidentally cut myself, I would not be surprised if, rather than blood, small "D" and "I" letters or perhaps letters spelling out diversity and inclusion, would emerge.

It is with this personal backdrop that I consider the 19th Amendment to the U.S. Constitution and its history, what progress we have made, and what we yet must do to close the gap between our ideals and our lived experiences, individually and collectively.

Historical Truths and the 19th Amendment

I am perplexed by the lack of acceptance of the truth of our history and how that lack of acceptance impacts laws and policy. In school, I was taught that, as a female, Susan B. Anthony should be one of my Sheroes because it was she, Elizabeth Cady Stanton, Lucretia Mott, Alice Paul, and a few others who helped me, as a woman, attain the right to vote. I was accepting of that notion. After all, that is what was written in the mainstream history textbooks and depicted in the women's suffrage statue prominently displayed in the U.S. Capitol building.[9]

---

8. *See, e.g.*, *1994 Election*, APARTHEID MUSEUM, https://www.apartheidmuseum.org/exhibitions/1994-election (last visited June 19, 2021).

9. *See Portrait Monument to Lucretia Mott, Elizabeth Cady Stanton and Susan B. Anthony*, ARCHITECT OF THE CAPITOL, U.S. CAPITOL (a 14,000-pound sculpture installed in the U.S. Capitol Rotunda in 1921 to commemorate the 19th Amendment and to educate the public about the role of these three women as leaders of the women's suffrage movement) https://www.aoc.gov/explore-capitol-campus/art

Throughout the years, false or incomplete narratives would find their way further into mainstream thinking, history books, and policies. The argument against the need for the Voting Rights Act of 1965 prohibiting racial discrimination because we already had voting rights ensured by the 15th[10] and 19th Amendments[11] is a classic example.

Fast forward to 2019 and everyone was talking about celebrating the 100th anniversary of the 19th Amendment in 2020. The celebration was short-lived, or it should have been. Alternatively, it could be said that the true purpose of the 19th Amendment has been revisited. As a matter of policy, we know facts have been intentionally omitted from history books, or partial facts have been provided, resulting in misinformation. And so, as we approached the centennial of the 19th Amendment, if it was to be celebrated at all, there had to be an understanding of all of the facts and what opportunities we as a country have missed because of policies embraced from a false or incomplete narrative.

Trailblazing Suffragists and Sheroes

As mentioned previously, when we think of the suffrage movement, we frequently think of, as mentioned earlier, Susan B. Anthony, Elizabeth Cady Stanton, Lucretia Mott, and Alice Paul as the primary leaders responsible for the enactment of the 19th Amendment. We think of them as courageous and even benevolent. It is a partial truth. The truth also includes formerly enslaved and freed Black women, including Sojourner Truth, Harriet Tubman, Maria W. Stewart, Henrietta Forten Purvis, Sarah Remond, and Mary Ann Shadd Cary[12] (the first woman law student at Howard University and the first Black/African American woman

---

/portrait-monument-lucretia-mott-elizabeth-cady-stanton-and-susan-b (last visited June 19, 2021).

10. U.S. Const. amend. XV § 1 (stating: "The right of citizens of the United States to vote shall not be denied or abridged by the United States or by any State on account of race, color, or previous condition of servitude.").

11. U.S. Const. amend. XIX § 1 (stating: "The right of citizens of the United States to vote shall not be denied or abridged by the United States or by any State on account of sex.").

12. *See* Sharon Harley, *African American Women and the Nineteenth Amendment*, Nat'l Park Serv., https://www.nps.gov/articles/african-american-women-and-the-nineteenth-amendment.htm (Apr. 19, 2019).

to actively recruit troops for the U.S. Army during the Civil War).[13] I would be remiss if I did not acknowledge the DuBois Circle of Baltimore and the members of my esteemed sorority, Delta Sigma Theta Incorporated. Both organizations and its members played a prominent role in the Suffrage movement, albeit not until the 1900s.

These prominent trailblazing Black/African American Sheroes of women's rights and suffrage in the 1800s recognized the power of collective action and the benefits of having other activists at their table. To that end, they strategically aligned their suffrage advocacy with prominent Black/African American men, including Frederick Douglass, Charles Lenox Remond, and Robert Purvis.[14] They also worked with slavery abolitionists, such as the wealthy Forten family, a prominent Black/African American family in Philadelphia known for financing and establishing numerous interracial anti-slavery and suffrage advocacy organizations.[15] Black/African American women and men also took active leadership roles in the American Equal Rights Association, founded in 1866 by Susan B. Anthony and Elizabeth Cady Stanton and dedicated to securing "Equal Rights to all American citizens, especially the right of suffrage, irrespective of race, color, or sex."[16]

That collaborative advocacy diminished with the passage of the 15th Amendment in 1869 and the following push for its ratification by the states. The lack of explicit language for equal suffrage for women was not well received by some women suffragists,[17] resulting in contentious divisions within the women's movement along strategic and racial lines. Notably, Anthony and Cady Stanton objected to uneducated Black/African American men potentially getting the right to vote before educated White women.[18]

---

13. *See* Jennifer Davis, *Mary Ann Shadd Cary: Lawyer, Educator, Suffragist*, *in* CUSTODIA LEGIS: LAW LIBRARIANS OF CONG., LIBRARY OF CONG. (Feb. 28, 2019), https://blogs.loc.gov/law/2019/02/mary-ann-shadd-cary-lawyer-educator-suffragist/.

14. *See* Harley, *supra* note 12.

15. *See Africans in America, Teacher's Guide Part 3: The Forten Women*, PBS, https://www.pbs.org/wgbh/aia/part3/3p477.html (last updated June 19, 2021).

16. *Making Good the Promises: 150 Years and Counting: The Struggle to Secure the Promise of the 15th Amendment*, NAT'L MUSEUM OF AFRICAN AM. HISTORY & CULTURE, https://nmaahc.si.edu/explore/exhibitions/reconstruction/voting-rights (last visited June 19, 2021).

17. *See id.*

18. *See* Harley, *supra* note 12.

In the independent advocacy publication owned by Anthony and edited by Cady Stanton, *The Revolution*, they derogatorily referred to former slaves as "Sambo" and disparaged poor immigrants, writing:

> Think of Patrick and Sambo and Hans and Yung Tung who do not know the difference between a Monarchy and a Republic, who never read the Declaration of Independence or Webster's spelling book, making laws for Lydia Maria Child, Lucretia Mott, or Fanny Kemble. . . . Would these gentlemen who, on all sides, are telling us "to wait until the negro is safe" be willing to stand aside and trust all *their* interests in hands like these?[19]

It is clear, although a New Yorker, Cady Stanton was not exempt from bigotry. Perhaps the fact that her family owned three slaves until New York abolished slavery in 1827 informs us of the rationale of her thinking.

While Cady Stanton was casting these aspersions, incredulously, she was simultaneously trying to infer the plight of White women was somehow greater than that of Black/African American men with the query: "[S]hall American statesmen . . . so amend their constitutions as to make their wives and mothers the political inferiors of unlettered and unwashed ditch-diggers, boot-blacks, butchers, and barbers, fresh from the slave plantations of the South, . . . ?"[20]

After listening to similar remarks by Cady Stanton at the American Equal Rights Association anniversary meeting at Steinway Hall in May of 1869 and acknowledging her purported commitment to civil rights, Frederick Douglass, responding to this notion as no other could, stated: "when women, because they are women, are hunted down through the cities of New York and New Orleans; when they are dragged from their houses and hung from lamp-posts; when their children are torn from their arms, and their brains dashed out upon the pavement; when they are objects of insult and rage at every turn; when they are in danger of having their homes burnt down . . . then they will have an urgency to obtain the ballot equal to our own."[21] Someone then asked Douglass, "Is that not

---

19. Susan B. Anthony, *Manhood Suffrage*, THE REVOLUTION, Dec. 24, 1868 (Elizabeth Cady Stanton & Parker Pillsbury eds.), at 7.

20. 2 SUSAN B. ANTHONY, HISTORY OF WOMAN SUFFRAGE 355 (Elizabeth Cady Stanton et al. eds. 1887) (quoting Elizabeth Cady Stanton's speech on the first evening of the National Woman's Suffrage Convention on January 19, 1869).

21. *Id.* at 382 (speaking at the American Equal Rights Association anniversary meeting at Steinway Hall, New York on May 12, 1869, which was chaired by Elizabeth Cady Stanton, the association's first vice president, in the absence of Lucretia Mott, the association's president).

all true about black women?"[22] Douglass replied, "Yes, yes, yes; it is true of the black woman, but not because she is a woman, but because she is black."[23]

Days later, Cady Stanton and Anthony formed the National Woman Suffrage Association (NWSA) and crusaded on a platform that White women were more deserving and qualified to vote than Black/African American men.[24] In contrast, the American Woman Suffrage Association (AWSA), formed in November 1869 by Lucy Stone and Julia Ward Howe, continued its support of the 15th Amendment and focused its advocacy on women's suffrage amendments at the state level, with the aim of lobbying for a constitutional amendment for women's suffrage after the ratification of the 15th Amendment.[25] The two national rivals later merged in 1890 to advance women's suffrage through an amendment to the U.S. Constitution and women's political equality.[26]

Without regard to this change in direction and the persistent anti-Black/African American rhetoric espoused by Anthony and Cady Stanton, Black/African American women were undaunted and forged ahead, forming suffrage groups and mobilizing support. This was a time of activism by Harriet Tubman, Helen Appo Cook, Sojourner Truth, Fanny Jackson Coppin, Anna Julia Cooper, Margaret Murray Washington, Naomi Bowman Talbert Anderson, Sarah Garnet, Victoria Earle Matthews, and so many others.

In 1896, when the president of a press association attempted to discredit renowned anti-lynching journalist Ida B. Wells-Barnett and made atrocious racist and derogatory remarks about Blacks/African Americans, Josephine St. Pierre Ruffin issued a national "Call to Confer" to various women's groups for solidarity in anti-racist advocacy, resulting in the merging of two major national organizations into the National Association of Colored Women (NACW).[27] Mary Church Terrell, born the same year as President Abraham Lincoln's Emancipation Proclamation and

---

22. *Id.*

23. *Id.*

24. *See* Harley, *supra* note 12.

25. *See, e.g.*, *Notable Women's Rights Leaders1800–1900: Lucy Stone: Women's Rights National Historical Park*, NAT'L PARK SERV., https://www.nps.gov/wori/learn/historyculture/lucy-stone.htm (last visited June 19, 2021).

26. *Archives & Manuscripts: National American Woman Suffrage Association Records*, NY PUB. LIBRARY, http://archives.nypl.org/mss/2097 (last visited June 19, 2021).

27. *About NACWC*, NAT'L ASS'N OF COLORED WOMEN, https://www.nacwc.com/history (last visited June 19, 2021).

one of the first Black/African American women to earn a college degree, became the organization's first president.[28] Their agenda was rarely single-issue, driving a progressive agenda and often combining political policy issues at the crossroads of race and gender with broader social and economic issues, including raising awareness of lynchings, poor prison conditions, and segregation.[29] They were courageous and persevering in their fight for human dignity and human rights for all human beings.

Yet, critical work by these Suffrage Sheroes and their goals of interracial advocacy cooperation were impeded, if not largely ignored, by White-dominated suffrage organizations.[30] During the first women's suffrage parade in Washington, D.C., in 1913, organized by the National American Woman Suffrage Association, Black/African American suffragists and their delegations were assigned by Alice Paul to march at the end of the parade, after the men, and were deliberately omitted from the program to avoid upsetting supporters from the South.[31] The country's largest civil rights association at the time, the National Association for the Advancement of Colored People (NAACP), reported that many Black/African American suffragists objected to the segregated parade and, despite attempts to segregate them, marched in their state delegations at the front of the parade.[32] Among them, Ida B. Wells-Barnett marched with the Illinois delegation flanked by her suffrage club cofounder Belle

28. *See* Jennifer Davis, *Mary Church Terrell, Suffragist and Civil Rights Activist*, *in* CUSTODIA LEGIS: LAW LIBRARIANS OF CONG., LIBRARY OF CONG. (Mar. 9, 2020) (earning her bachelor's and master's degrees at Oberlin College in 1884 and later successfully legal challenging racial segregation in restaurants in Washington, D.C., including the landmark U.S. Supreme Court case of District of Columbia v. Thompson Co., 346 U.S. 100 (1953)), https://blogs.loc.gov/law/2020/03/mary-church-terrell-suffragist-and-civil-rights-activist/.

29. *See* Martha S. Jones, *How Black Suffragists Fought for the Right to Vote and a Modicum of Respect*, 40 HUMANITY 3 (Summer 2019), https://www.neh.gov/article/how-black-suffragists-fought-right-vote-and-modicum-respect.

30. *Cf. Sarah J. Garnet*, NAT'L PARK SERV., https://www.nps.gov/people/sarah-j-garnet.htm (last updated Mar. 11, 2021).

31. *See* Rebecca Boggs Roberts, *The Great Suffrage Parade of 1913*, NAT'L PARK SERV., https://www.nps.gov/articles/000/the-great-suffrage-parade-of-1913.htm (last updated Dec. 14, 2020).

32. *See Politics*, 5 THE CRISIS 268 (W.E. Burghardt Du Bois et al. eds., Apr. 1913), https://transcription.si.edu/view/35305/NMAAHC-2015_97_14_6_005.

Squire and Virginia Brooks.[33] Mary Church Terrell marched in her cap and gown.[34]

A little-known truth is that, because voting practices were states' rights long before 1920, millions of White women had the right to vote in several states and did indeed vote before the ratification of the 19th Amendment.[35] Thus, what women "technically" won was a constitutional protection against discrimination on the basis of "sex."[36] In practice, the 19th Amendment enabled millions more women, largely White woman, the right and ability to vote.[37] Yet, for millions of Black/African Americans, the right to vote remained elusive due to state and local laws enforcing racial segregation and discrimination against Black/African Americans, known as "Black Codes" or "Jim Crow" laws.[38]

As historian Lisa Tretrault describes:

> Discriminatory laws kept women of color from voting in the north and west as well. During the early 1900s, native-born whites in both regions worked to "purify" the electorate of "problem voters," which largely meant immigrants and voters of color. Numerous northern and western states expanded their residency requirements for voting, tightened registration requirements, and shortened registration windows. Twelve northern and western states—from New York to California—also added literacy tests to their state requirements for voting. Like those in the south, these tests were often selectively administered against voters of color, including women. Yet because neither "race" nor

---

33. *See* Paula J. Giddings, *A Noble Endeavor: Ida B. Wells-Barnett and Suffrage*, NAT'L PARK SERV., https://www.nps.gov/articles/000/a-noble-endeavor-ida-b-wells-barnett-and-suffrage.htm (last updated Dec. 14, 2020).

34. *See 1913 Woman Suffrage Procession*, NAT'L PARK SERV., https://www.nps.gov/articles/woman-suffrage-procession1913.htm (last updated Dec. 15, 2020).

35. *See, e.g., Did Women Earn the Right to Vote on August 18, 1920? Ulysses S. Grant National Historic Site*, NAT'L PARK SERV., https://www.nps.gov/articles/000/did-women-earn-the-right-to-vote-on-august-18-1920.htm (last updated Jan. 25, 2021).

36. U.S. CONST. amend. XIX; Lisa Tetrault, *Winning the Vote: A Divided Movement Brought About the Nineteenth Amendment*, 40 HUMANITIES 3 (Summer 2019), https://www.neh.gov/article/winning-vote-divided-movement-brought-about-nineteenth-amendment.

37. *See Did Women Earn the Right to Vote on August 18, 1920? Ulysses S. Grant National Historic Site*, *supra* note 35.

38. *See Classroom Materials: Primary Source Set: Jim Crow and Segregation*, LIBRARY OF CONG., https://www.loc.gov/classroom-materials/jim-crow-segregation/ (last visited June 19, 2021).

> "sex" was mentioned in the letter of these laws, they were also perfectly constitutional. Still others, particularly Asian, Pacific Islander, and indigenous women, were barred from voting by restrictions on their citizenship.[39]

Black/African American women were not alone in being left out by White women. Native American women also faced challenges. As a result, prominent Native Americans who were concerned not only about voting rights but also, of all things, citizenship, formed a group known as the Society of American Indians (SAI) and lobbied Congress and the Indian Service on these fundamental rights.[40] The Indian Citizenship Act of 1924 gave Native American men and women full citizenship and the right to vote, on paper.[41] The reality was continued resistance against Native Americans. Just as Black/African Americans were treated, literacy tests and poll taxes were used as impediments to Indigenous voters.

Unresolved Accomplishments

Ultimately, the Voting Rights Act of 1965 sought to strengthen legal protections for Black/African American voters, ostensibly resolving the issues of all women having the ability to vote, including Black/African American women and other women of color. For a time, the Voting Rights Act was relatively successful. The ratification of the 26th Amendment, lowering the voting age to 18, also expanded the right to vote.[42]

As has been demonstrated time and again, sadly, there has been no complete resolution of the 19th Amendment. We see its unresolved nature being played out in recent elections and as a result of recent elections.

As a result of the perceived successes attained, in 2020, we find ourselves in a replay of the dark side of history. It is clear that, while the right to vote has been bolstered by the 15th, 19th, 24th, and 26th Amendments and the federal Voting Rights Act of 1965, there are those who are determined to upend, if not reverse, these significant strides. That process is actively underway.[43] In April 2021, leaders of 62 of the country's top law

39. Tetrault, *supra* note 36.

40. *See Society of American Indians*, NAT'L ARCHIVES, https://www.archives.gov/nhprc/projects/catalog/society-of-american-indians (last visited June 19, 2021).

41. Indian Citizenship Act of 1924, ch. 233, 43 Stat. 253 (1924) (codified at 8 U.S.C. § 1401(b)).

42. U.S. CONST. amend. XXVI.

43. Vishal Agraharkar, *50 Years Later, Voting Rights Act Under Unprecedented Assault*, BRENNAN CTR. FOR JUSTICE (Aug. 2, 2015), https://www.brennancenter

firms signed a statement denouncing "all efforts to restrict the constitutional right of every eligible American to vote and to participate in our democracy," such as through new state laws restricting voting access.[44]

The statement says:

> Equal access to voting is a fundamental right in the United States. Making voting easier, not harder, for all eligible voters should be the goal of every elected official. Election laws that impose unnecessary obstacles and barriers on the right to vote and that disenfranchise underrepresented groups represent a significant step backwards for all Americans. Now, more than ever, courageous leadership is required from our elected officials.[45]

Further, with all but three states considering election legislation containing discriminatory voting measures after the 2020 U.S. elections, more than 500 major U.S. and global companies signed a statement in support of voting rights organized by the Black Economic Alliance.[46] The statement says: "Voting is the lifeblood of our democracy and we call upon all Americans to join us in taking a nonpartisan stand for this most basic and fundamental right of all Americans."[47]

Tomorrow's Trailblazing Sheroes

Although the 19th Amendment may be worthy of celebrating, the fundamental voting rights it intended to confer and women's full inclusion in political life and society remain unresolved. Until all impediments are removed to voting, and there is inclusion in the process of ensuring democracy and political participation for everyone, continuous vigilance is required. The work is not yet finished.

In 2021, it is devastating that there is no shortage of news of gender and other societal inequities in the United States and around the world. We cannot roll back hard-fought progress. Like the courageous women

---

.org/our-work/research-reports/50-years-later-voting-rights-act-under-unprecedented-assault.

44. *See* Debra Cassens Weiss, *Leaders of 62 BigLaw Firms Denounce Voting Restrictions; Coalition Is Formed to Challenge Legislation*, ABA J. (Apr. 13, 2021, 12:06 PM CDT), https://www.abajournal.com/news/article/leaders-of-62-biglaw-firms-denounce-voting-restrictions-coalition-is-formed-to-challenge-legislation.

45. *Id.*

46. *See We Stand for Democracy*, Black Econ. Alliance (Apr. 14, 2021), https://blackeconomicalliance.org/news/we-stand-for-democracy/.

47. *Id.*

before us, Black/African American women and other women of color are undaunted and are playing a prominent role in current day elections, combatting voter suppression laws, as leaders, advocates, and agitators, achieving significant positive results. Like Ida B. Wells-Barnett, we will not go to the back of the line or in time. Nor will we give up on our drive to strengthen the interconnectedness of our diverse, vibrant, and multicultural communities.

We are in a critical time for fulfilling the promise of women's equality and full inclusion in society, whereby each of us needs to be both intentional and vigilant, investing in our goals and our collective future. Women's political inclusion is more than just voting and getting enough room for a foot in the door. It is about ensuring more women, including women of color, have a meaningful seat at the decision-making table, before decisions are made, where their contributions and unique perspectives are valued.

Making progress on the unresolved achievements will require having courageous women (and perhaps a few good men) step forward as ethical and transformative trailblazers, leaders, and Sheroes.

Importantly, stand up for what you believe in and speak your mind. There is no time or place for bystanders.

12

United States: Personal Reflections on Lessons from the 19th Amendment to the U.S. Constitution

Gail Heriot Silverman[1]

My mother, Mary Rider Heriot (1921–2019), died the year before the 100th anniversary of the 19th Amendment to the U.S. Constitution, granting women the right to vote, in 2020. She was almost 98, dealing with dementia and the worn-down physicality of living too long in a body designed for a shorter life. She was still railing about the injustices in the world and dreaming of equal rights for all.

I am at least a fourth-generation American feminist. I grew up steeped in the concepts of social justice and equality for all. My mother and grandmothers, and my father as well, shared a painful understanding that the playing field was not all that level for women. I was always aware that women's right to vote was not original to our constitution but rather "granted" at a later date.

My grandmothers, both born in the 1890s, spoke about "winning" the right to vote and how they felt at their first elections. I grew up knowing that, for each, the right to vote produced a sense of citizenship and pride. Their first votes, as well as those that followed, were profound events with special meaning and significance.

My grandmothers spoke, also though, about the need to support their families, especially during the Depression. They were well familiar with the criticism that hiring a married woman would take a job away from a

1. Gail Heriot Silverman is a retired attorney and former member of the Judge Advocate General's Department in the U.S. Air Force. Her active duty service ended in 1982, and she continued her service as a member of the U.S. Air Force Reserve, retiring in 2004 in the grade of colonel.

man with a family. My maternal grandmother was particularly distressed when she applied for a teaching position during the Depression only to be told that they could not legally hire a married woman, even if her family had no other means of support. She and my mother knew, and frequently reminded me, that voting was critically important, but not the total answer.

Growing up in the 1950s and the 1960s, I was encouraged to read biographies of Lucretia Mott, Susan B. Anthony, Elizabeth Cady Stanton, and other women whose significant contributions to our society were not part of my mainstream education. I knew their stories, their struggles, and their successes. I did not know that many of those struggles survived. I thought I understood the world, but it was still a world with unwritten rules and limited perspectives and opportunities. I had finished college, was teaching elementary school, and pursuing a graduate degree before I ever met a woman lawyer. The following week, I signed up for the Law School Admission Test. Because my mother became immediately and fully committed to the renewal of the feminist movement in the 1970s, I was fortunately included.

The 19th Amendment states:

The right of the citizens of the United States to vote shall not be denied or abridged by the United States or by any State on account of sex.

Congress shall have the power to enforce this article by appropriate legislation.

As we celebrate the 100th anniversary of the adoption of the 19th Amendment to the U.S. Constitution, granting the right to vote to women, we have an opportunity to examine and take stock of its impact on women's lives and our overall national commitment to equality. Understanding the 19th Amendment's place in history starts with fully accepting the fact that the U.S. Constitution, as originally written and ratified, did not include women. Previous opportunities to include women under the constitution or to clarify their role as part of the electorate (as in the adoption of the 15th Amendment) were consciously avoided. We were not merely overlooked but rather purposefully omitted because of our perceived inferiority.

The American desire for gender equality did not begin with the 19th Amendment. It has always been with us, even at the very formation of our country. Abigail Adams (for whom I am named) famously summed it up in a letter to her husband, John, dated March 31, 1776:

> If perticular care and attention is not paid to the Laidies we are determined to foment a Rebelion, and will not hold ourselves bound by any Laws in which we have no voice, or Representation.[2]

The future president responded of course, displaying the diplomacy for which he became known. The formation of our government did not appear to have been benefited much by Abigail Adams's prodigious foresight.

We generally consider the American movement for women's right to vote to have been formally launched in Seneca Falls, New York, in 1848. A convention, called by Elizabeth Cady Stanton and Lucretia Mott, produced the "Declaration of Sentiments" in which Stanton and Mott list a substantial number of disenfranchising grievances or "usurpations," including:

- He has never permitted her to exercise her inalienable right to the elective franchise.
- He has compelled her to submit to laws, in the formation of which she had no voice.
- Having deprived her of this first right of a citizen, the elective franchise, thereby leaving her without representation in the halls of legislation, he has oppressed her on all sides.[3]

Among the many resolutions adopted is:

- Resolved, That it is the duty of the women of this country to secure to themselves their sacred right to the elective franchise.

Securing this "sacred" right was not easy, nor was it speedy.[4]

Much of the objection to suffrage, as well as other legal rights for women, was couched in the assertion that women needed to be protected from the harshness of the real world. Former slave Sojourner Truth's 1851 speech, "Ain't I a Woman," reminded all that non-White and less privileged women were discounted even more, with no hope of the social

---

2. Letter from Abigail Adams to John Adams (Mar. 31, 1776) (on file with U.S. Nat'l Archives & Records Admin.), https://founders.archives.gov/documents/Adams/04-01-02-0241.

3. *Declaration of Sentiments and Resolutions* in 1 Elizabeth Cady Stanton, Susan B. Anthony, and M.J. Cage. A History of Woman Suffrage (1889), https://www.womenshistory.org/resources/primary-source/declaration-sentiments-and-resolution.

4. *Id.*

courtesies or "protections" that purported to be fair substitutions for equal legal status.[5]

As the suffrage movement grew, many noteworthy women joined the cause. Among them were Susan B. Anthony, Mary Ann Shadd Cary, Carrie Chapman Catt, Lucretia Mott, Alice Paul, Elizabeth Cady Stanton, Lucy Stone, and Ida B. Wells-Barnett. These leaders differed some on their approaches and whether a state-by-state strategy, as opposed to a constitutional amendment, would yield faster results. They differed as well on the level of militancy required to achieve their goals. Although a few states did extend the right to vote to women, the majority of suffragists chose to pursue the constitutional change.

When we casually discuss when women were "given" the right to vote, or when the right was "granted," or even the adoption of the 19th Amendment, it sounds rather neat and tidy. The truth is far different. This was not a grant or a gift, but rather a hard-fought and brutal battle for an essential American right. Though we envision gentle parades of suffragists attired in white, speeches, petitions, and mild civil disobediences, there were also cruel verbal and physical attacks, imprisonments, and hunger strikes. Alice Paul, in particular, suffered greatly from the abuses, forced feedings, and threats of institutionalization.

Suffragists frequently came from the ranks of abolitionists. It must have been a crushing disappointment for many of them that the proposed post–Civil War amendments to the constitution did not contemplate including women in their scope. The 15th Amendment, which granted freed and formerly enslaved African American men the right to vote, was ratified in 1870, a full 50 years before women gained that right. Technically, the 15th Amendment granted the right of "citizens" to vote without regard to "race, color, or previous condition of servitude,"[6] but the common understanding, including that of the courts, was that women were not included.

Arguably the 19th Amendment was only the first goal along the pathway to full legal and constitutional equality for women. Indeed, it is feminist folklore that the full legal inclusion of women under the U.S. Constitution was always the ultimate goal, and that suffrage was an important milestone along the way. Returning to the Seneca Falls "Declaration of Sentiments," one finds substantial support for this theory,

5. Sojourner Truth, *Women's Rights Convention*, 6 ANTI-SLAVERY BUGLE 160, June 21, 1851, https://chroniclingamerica.loc.gov/lccn/sn83035487/1851-06-21/ed-1/seq-4/.

6. U.S. CONST. amend. XV.

including this language: "The history of mankind is a history of repeated injuries and usurpations on the part of man toward woman, having in direct object the establishment of an absolute tyranny over her."[7]

Individual grievances were enumerated that noted:

- Married women were "in the eye of the law, civilly dead";
- The laws of divorce were based on a "false supposition of the supremacy of man";
- Women were denied opportunities for education;
- Society closed "avenues to wealth and distinction" to women; and
- "A false public sentiment" produced a double moral standard for men and women.[8]

Thus, it is clear that early feminists were insisting upon much more than the right to vote. Among their 12 resolutions, we find:

- Resolved, That all laws which prevent woman from occupying such a station in society as her conscience shall dictate, or which place her in a position inferior to that of man, are contrary to the great precept of nature, and therefore of no force or authority.
- Resolved, That woman is man's equal—was intended to be so by the Creator, and the highest good of the race demands that she should be recognized as such. . . .
- Resolved, That the speedy success of our cause depends upon the zealous and untiring efforts of both men and women . . . and for the securing to woman an equal participation with men in the various trades, professions, and commerce.[9]

Alice Paul, a suffragist with extensive involvement in the effort for the vote in both the United Kingdom and the United States, lost no time in moving forward. She is credited as the author of the Equal Rights Amendment.[10]

The Equal Rights Amendment states:

> Section 1. Equality of Rights under the law shall not be denied or abridged by the United States or any State on account of sex.

---

7. *Declaration of Sentiments and Resolutions*, *supra* note 3.
8. *Id.*
9. *Id.*
10. *The Equal Rights Amendment: A Brief History*, Alice Paul Inst. (2019), https://www.alicepaul.org/equal-rights-amendment-2; *cf.* Equal Rights Amendment, H.R.J. Res. 75, 68th Cong. (1st Sess. 1923).

Section 2. The Congress shall have the power to enforce, by appropriate legislation, the provisions of this article.

Section 3. This amendment shall take effect two years after the date of ratification.[11]

As early as 1923, the Equal Rights Amendment was introduced in Congress. In fact, it was introduced continuously until its passage in 1972. Senate objections resulted in a time limitation for ratification, and, although the required number of states have ratified, Congress must now take action to remove the time constraint.

Full acceptance of women as equal citizens and contributors to our society certainly raises the issue of military service. For men, military service has not always been voluntary and still requires a coming of age registration. Women serving in the military services is, of course, not a new idea. There have always been women serving with or in our military. My mother, in her testimony supporting the Equal Rights Amendment before the South Carolina Senate Judiciary Committee in 1972, described her own service as a U.S. Army nurse in the South Pacific during World War II. Although she readily admitted that she would not want to go through those experiences again, she noted: "I look back with a sense of satisfaction—knowing that I have made some contribution toward our cherished way of life." Feminists were always asked by opponents about their feelings on their daughters being drafted. My mother's answer was that she did not want to see her daughter drafted, but she always added that "I do not want to see my sons drafted either."

What she did not say, and I came to understand only shortly before her death, was that her own mother had encouraged her to volunteer for U.S. Army service. She was a newly graduated nurse in 1942, and my grandmother reminded her that her brother, Sam, was signing up and that she should too. Needless to say, my own military service decades later was fairly well received. That the benefits and responsibilities of full citizenship should go hand in hand is self-evident. While military service was viewed by some as a threat imposed by the Equal Rights Amendment (ERA) in the 1970s, women's role in the military is now recognized as crucial to the defense of our country and advantageous to those women looking for career choices and educational benefits. Additionally, even without the ERA, Congress could change the Selective Service statute to include women if the need would arise, and indeed had contemplated doing that during World War II.

11. Equal Rights Amendment, H.R.J. Res. 208, 92nd Cong. (1972).

As my mother's daughter, I had the opportunity to participate in the 1970s effort for the Equal Rights Amendment. I met many of the women I most admired and learned to trust and believe in myself. Over the years, I have watched women make impressive progress on many fronts. Nevertheless, we know that many women still find their lives burdened by unequal and uncomfortable treatment, at home and at work. We have only to look at the "Me Too" movement and the domestic violence statistics to realize that we have more work to do in resolving the gender divide.

As we recognize the centennial anniversary of the 19th Amendment, we are dealing with a pandemic, quarantines, and economic uncertainty. We are experiencing a political climate, on all sides, identified by neither its civility nor intellectual rigor. Amidst this disruption, as we rebuild and restore our educational, economic, and political processes, I am left with my mother's lingering concern: "Aren't we only halfway there? Shouldn't women finally be fully included in the United States Constitution?" To my mind, the only fitting way to recognize and celebrate the 100th anniversary of the 19th Amendment is to adopt the long-pending Equal Rights Amendment.